PENGUIN POPULAR REFERENCE

ITALIAN PHRASE BOOK

D1166068

SECOND EDITION

Pietro Giorgetti and
Jill Norman

Italian
Phrase
Book

PENGUIN BOOKS

Published by the Penguin Group
Penguin Books Ltd, 80 Strand, London WC2R ORL, England
Penguin Putnam Inc., 375 Hudson Street, New York, New York 10014, USA
Penguin Books Australia Ltd, Ringwood, Victoria, Australia
Penguin Books Canada Ltd, 10 Alcorn Avenue, Toronto, Ontario, Canada M4V 3B2
Penguin Books India (P) Ltd, 11 Community Centre, Panchsheel Park,
New Delhi – 110 017, India
Penguin Books (NZ) Ltd, Cnr Rosedale and Airborne Roads, Albany, Auckland,
New Zealand
Penguin Books (South Africa) (Pty) Ltd, 24 Sturdee Avenue, Rosebank 2196, South Africa

Penguin Books Ltd, Registered Offices: 80 Strand, London WC2R ORL, England

www.penguin.com

First published 1968
Second edition 1979
12

Copyright © Jill Norman and Pietro Giorgetti, 1968, 1979
All rights reserved

Printed in England by Cox & Wyman Ltd, Reading, Berkshire

Contents

6 Contents

8 Contents

Introduction

In this series of phrase books only those words and phrases that are essential to the traveller have been included. For easy reference the phrases are divided into several sections, each one dealing with a different situation.

*Some of the Italian phrases are marked with an asterisk – these attempt to give an indication of the kind of reply you may get to your questions.

At the end of the book is an extensive vocabulary list and here a pronunciation guide is given for each word. In addition there is an explanation of Italian pronunciation at the beginning of the book and a brief survey of the essential points of grammar. It would be advisable to read these sections before starting to use the book.

For those who would like to study the phrases and perfect their pronunciation, a further aid is available in the form of two 90-minute cassettes which contain all the words and phrases spoken clearly and distinctly by Italian men and women.

A leaflet giving full details is available from the Institute of Tape Learning, P.O. Box 4, Hemel Hempstead, Hertfordshire (telephone 0442 68484).

Pronunciation

The pronunciation guide is intended for people with no knowledge of Italian. As far as possible the system is based on English pronunciation. This means that complete accuracy may sometimes be lost for the sake of simplicity, but the reader should be able to understand Italian pronunciation, and make himself understood, if he reads this section carefully. In addition, each word in the vocabulary and in the word lists that occur in some sections is given with a pronunciation guide.

VOWELS

All vowels are sounded distinctly; unstressed vowels keep their pure sound and are never slurred as in English. Final 'e' is always sounded.

Pronounce:	a as a in father	Symbol a	e.g. pane – bread (pa-nay)
	e as e in eight	Symbol ay	e.g. ponte – bridge (pon-tay)
and	e as e in wet	Symbol e or ai	e.g. mezzo – half (med-zoh)
	i as i in machine	Symbol ee	e.g. litro – litre (lee-troh)

	o as o in open	Symbol o(h)	e.g. presto – soon (pres-toh)
and	o as o in soft	Symbol o	e.g. opera – opera (op-air-a)
	u as oo in moon	Symbol oo	e.g. punto – point (poon-toh)

COMPOUND VOWELS

In the combinations ie, io, iu the i tends to be shortened and sounds rather like y in yet. This is shown as y or ee in the pronunciation guide, e.g. pensione – boarding house (pens-yo-nay), piede – foot (pee-e-day).

In the combinations ue, ui, uo the u sounds like w in wet and is represented by w or oo in the pronunciation guide, e.g. guida – guide (gwee-da), buono – good (bwon-oh).

Au is like ow in how, e.g. paura – fear (pow-ra).

CONSONANTS

In general consonants are pronounced much as in English, although r is always pronounced very distinctly. Note the following:

c followed by e or i is pronounced as ch in church	Symbol ch	e.g. cibo – food (chee-boh)
c followed by a, o, u is pronounced as k in king	Symbol k	e.g. casa – house (ka-sa)
g followed by e or i is pronounced as j in joy	Symbol j	e.g. gente – people (jen-tay)
g followed by a, o, u is pronounced as g in good	Symbol g	e.g. gatto – cat (gat-toh)

s has two sounds – as in taste and in nose. Symbols s and z are used respectively, e.g. sigaro – cigar (**see**-ga-roh) and rosa – rose (ro-za).

z also has two sounds – ts as in cuts and ds as in birds. Symbols ts (tz) and dz, e.g. zio – uncle (tsee-oh) and mezzo – half (med-zoh).

GROUPS OF CONSONANTS

Double consonants, like cc, gg always represent a single but more heavily stressed sound.

The following groups also represent a single sound:

ch is pronounced k as in king	Symbol k	e.g. chiesa – church (kee-e-za)
gh is pronounced g as in good	Symbol g(h)	e.g. ghiaccio – ice (ghee-ach-yo)
gl followed by i is like lli of million	Symbol ly	e.g. figlio – son (feel-yo)
gn is like ni of onion	Symbol ny	e.g. bagno – bath (ban-yo)
sc followed by e or i is pronounced sh as in ship	Symbol sh	e.g. sciarpa – scarf (shar-pa)
sc followed by a, o, u is pronounced sk	Symbol sk	e.g. scuola – school (skwo-la)

STRESS

Most Italian words are stressed on the next to last syllable. If the last syllable is stressed it is written with an accent. Irregular stress is indicated in the pronunciation guide by printing the stressed syllable in **bold type**.

Basic grammar

NOUNS

All Italian nouns are either masculine or feminine. Almost all nouns ending in **-o** are *masculine* [e.g. ragazzo – boy, biglietto – ticket]. Most nouns ending in **-a** are *feminine* [e.g. ragazza – girl, cartolina – postcard]. Those ending in **-e** are masculine or feminine (e.g. melone – melon *m*, stazione – station *f*].

PLURAL

Nouns ending in **-o** change to **-i** in the plural [e.g. ragazzi – boys, biglietti – tickets].

Nouns ending in **-a** change to **-e** [e.g. ragazze – girls, cartoline – postcards].

Nouns ending in **-e** change to **-i** whether they are masculine or feminine [e.g. meloni – melons, stazioni – stations].

   N.B. An exception: the plural of uomo is uomini [man, men].

THE ARTICLES

The articles change form to match the gender of the noun, and the definite article has a plural as well as a singular form.

'A' before a *masculine noun* is **un** unless the noun begins with **s** followed by a consonant, or **z**, when it is **uno** [e.g. un uomo – a man, un giornale – a newspaper, but uno zio – an uncle, uno specchio – a mirror]. 'A' before a *feminine noun* is **una** unless the noun begins with a vowel, when it is shortened to **un'** [e.g. una donna – a woman, but un'avventura – an adventure].

'The' with *masculine singular nouns* is usually **il** [e.g. il ragazzo – the boy]. But it is **lo** before a word beginning with **s** + consonant, or **z** [e.g. lo specchio – the mirror, lo zio – the uncle]. It becomes **l'** before a vowel [e.g. l'anno – the year].

'The' before a *masculine plural noun* is generally **i** [e.g. i giorni – the days]. But it is **gli** before a word beginning with **s**+consonant, **z** or a vowel [e.g. gli specchi – the mirrors, gli uomini – the men].

'The' before a *feminine singular noun* is **la**, shortened to **l'** if the noun begins with a vowel [e.g. la madre – the mother, l'opera – the opera]. With *feminine nouns in the plural* 'the' is **le** [e.g. le case – the houses].

ADJECTIVES

Adjectives end either in **-o** or in **-e**. Those ending in **-o** form the feminine by changing to **-a**; those ending in **-e** are the same in both genders.

All adjectives form their plural in the same way as nouns: **-o** changes to **-i**; **-a** to **-e**; **-e** to **-i**.

	Sing.	Plu.	
m	rosso	rossi	red
f	rossa	rosse	
m	verde	verdi	green
f	verde	verdi	

Adjectives have the same gender and number as the nouns they qualify, and they sometimes follow the noun [e.g. un ragazzo intelligente – due ragazzi intelligenti].

POSSESSIVE ADJECTIVES

Sing.			Plu.	
m	f		m	f
mio	mia	*my*	miei	mie
tuo	tua	*your*	tuoi	tue
suo	sua	*his, her, its*	suoi	sue
nostro	nostra	*our*	nostri	nostre
vostro	vostra	*your*	vostri	vostre
loro	loro	*their*	loro	loro

Possessive adjectives are usually preceded by the definite article [e.g. la mia macchina – my car, la nostra casa – our house, i suoi fratelli – his brothers].

YOU

The polite form of address in Italian is in the third person. 'You' is translated by **Lei** if addressing one person; **Loro** if addressing more than one. 'Your' is **Suo** (sing.) and **Loro** (plu.). **Tu** is only used to a close friend or a child.

e.g. Come sta (Lei)? How are you? Come stanno i Suoi figli? How are your children?

VERBS

Essere – *to be*

Present		*Future*	
io sono	I am	io sarò	I shall be
tu sei	you are	tu sarai	you will be
egli/essa è	he/she is	egli/essa sarà	he/she will be
Lei è	you are	Lei sarà	you will be
noi siamo	we are	noi saremo	we shall be
voi siete	you are	voi sarete	you will be
essi/esse		essi/esse	
sono	they are	saranno	they will be
Loro sono	you are	Loro saranno	you will be

Past

io sono stato	I was *or* I have been, etc.
tu sei stato	you were
egli/essa è stato/(-a)	he/she was
Lei è stato/(-a)	you were
noi siamo stati/(-e)	we were
voi siete stati/(-e)	you were
essi/esse sono stati/(-e)	they were
Loro sono stati/(-e)	you were

Avere – *to have*

Present		*Future*	
io ho	I have	io avrò	I shall have
tu hai	you have	tu avrai	you will have
egli/essa ha	he/she has	egli/essa avrà	he/she will have

Lei ha	you have	Lei avrà	you will have
noi abbiamo	we have	noi avremo	we shall have
voi avete	you have	voi avrete	you will have
essi/esse hanno	they have	essi/esse avranno	they will have
Loro hanno	you have	Loro avranno	you will have

Past

io ho avuto	I had	*or*	I have had, etc.
tu hai avuto	you had		
egli/essa ha avuto	he/she had		
Lei ha avuto	you had		
noi abbiamo avuto	we had		
voi avete avuto	you had		
essi/esse hanno avuto	they had		
Loro hanno avuto	you had		

REGULAR VERBS

Italian regular verbs fall into three conjugations, determined by the ending of the infinitive.

1st conjugation	infinitives ending in -are	e.g. parlare – to speak
		comprare – to buy
2nd conjugation	infinitives ending in -ere	e.g. vedere – to see
		vendere – to sell
3rd conjugation	infinitives ending in -ire	e.g. sentire – to hear
		capire – to understand

Present tense

	1st conj.	*2nd conj.*	*3rd conj.*
io	parl-**o**	vend-**o**	sent-**o**
tu	parl-**i**	vend-**i**	sent-**i**

1st conj.	2nd conj.	3rd conj.
egli parl-**a**	vend-**e**	sent-**e**
Lei parl-**a**	vend-**e**	sent-**e**
noi parl-**iamo**	vend-**iamo**	sent-**iamo**
voi parl-**ate**	vend-**ete**	sent-**ite**
essi parl-**ano**	vend-**ono**	sent-**ono**
Loro parl-**ano**	vend-**ono**	sent-**ono**

Some 3rd conjugation verbs add -**isc** before the normal present tense endings in the singular and in the third person plural, e.g. io capisco, from capire – to understand.

Future tense

The future tense of almost all Italian verbs is formed from the infinitive in the following way:

io	parl-er-**ò**	vend-er-**ò**	sent-ir-**ò**
tu	parl-er-**ai**	vend-er-**ai**	sent-ir-**ai**
egli	parl-er-**à**	vend-er-**à**	sent-ir-**à**
Lei	parl-er-**à**	vend-er-**à**	sent-ir-**à**
noi	parl-er-**emo**	vend-er-**emo**	sent-ir-**emo**
voi	parl-er-**ete**	vend-er-**ete**	sent-ir-**ete**
essi	parl-er-**anno**	vend-er-**anno**	sent-ir-**anno**

Note that in the 1st conjugation -are changes to -ere before the future endings are added.

Past tense

The form of the past tense given in this book can be used to translate the English 'I did (something)' as well as 'I have done (something)'. It is formed by using the present tense of avere, or sometimes essere, with the past participle of the verb.

When essere – to be – is used to form the past tense, past participles agree with the subject of the verb in number and gender, using the same endings as adjectives ending in -o. E.g. Maria è venuta – Maria has come; I miei amici sono andati a Roma – My friends have gone to Rome.

The past participle of 1st conjugation verbs ends in **-ato** [e.g. parlato].

The past participle of 2nd conjugation verbs usually ends in **-uto** [e.g. venduto].

The past participle of 3rd conjugation verbs usually ends in **-ito** [e.g. sentito].

The past tense is formed as follows:

io ho parlato, etc.   io ho venduto, etc.   io ho sentito, etc.

SOME COMMON IRREGULAR VERBS

Andare – *to go*

Present		*Future*	
io vado	I go, etc.	io andrò	I shall go, etc.
tu vai		tu andrai	
egli va		egli andrà	
Lei va		Lei andrà	
noi andiamo		noi andremo	
voi andate		voi andrete	
essi vanno		essi andranno	
Loro vanno		Loro andranno	

Past

io sono andato   I went/have been, etc.

Dire – *to say*

Present		*Future*	
io dico	I say, etc.	io dirò	I shall say, etc.
tu dici		tu dirai	
egli dice		egli dirà	
Lei dice		Lei dirà	
noi diciamo		noi diremo	
voi dite		voi direte	
essi dicono		essi diranno	
Loro dicono		Loro diranno	

Past

Io ho detto   I said/have said, etc.

Dovere – *to have to, must*

Present		*Future*	
io debbo	I have to, etc.	io dovrò	I shall have to, etc.
tu devi		tu dovrai	
egli deve		egli dovrà	
Lei deve		Lei dovrà	
noi dobbiamo		noi dovremo	
voi dovete		voi dovrete	
essi devono		essi dovranno	
Loro devono		Loro dovranno	

Past

io ho dovuto   I had to/have had to, etc.

Fare – *to do, to make*

Present		Future	
io faccio	I do, etc.	io farò	I shall do, etc.
tu fai		tu farai	
egli fa		egli farà	
Lei fa		Lei farà	
noi facciamo		noi faremo	
voi fate		voi farete	
essi fanno		essi faranno	
Loro fanno		Loro faranno	

Past

io ho fatto   I did/have done, etc.

Potere – *to be able to, can*

Present		Future	
io posso	I can, etc.	io potrò	I shall be able to, etc.
tu puoi		tu potrai	
egli può		egli potrà	
Lei può		Lei potrà	
noi possiamo		noi potremo	
voi potete		voi potrete	
essi possono		essi potranno	
Loro possono		Loro potranno	

Past

io ho potuto   I could/was able to, etc.

Venire – *to come*

Present		*Future*	
io vengo	I come, etc.	io verrò	I shall come, etc.
tu vieni		tu verrai	
egli viene		egli verrà	
Lei viene		Lei verrà	
noi veniamo		noi verremo	
voi venite		voi verrete	
essi vengono		essi verranno	
Loro vengono		Loro verranno	

Past

io sono venuto   I came/have come, etc.

Volere – *to want*

Present
io voglio   I want, etc.
tu vuoi
egli vuole
Lei vuole
noi vogliamo
voi volete
essi vogliono
Loro vogliono

Past

io ho voluto   I wanted/have wanted, etc.

PREPOSITIONS

The most common prepositions are:

a, ad	*at, to*	in	*in, to*
di	*of*	su	*on, over*
da	*from*	con	*with*

When they are followed by the definite article they are joined to it as follows:

	il	*lo*	*l'*	*la*	*i*	*gli*	*le*
a	al	allo	all'	alla	ai	agli	alle
di	del	dello	dell'	della	dei	degli	delle
da	dal	dallo	dall'	dalla	dai	dagli	dalle
in	nel	nello	nell'	nella	nei	negli	nelle
su	sul	sullo	sull'	sulla	sui	sugli	sulle
con	col	collo	coll'	colla	coi	cogli	colle

e.g. al mercato – to the market; nel giardino – in the garden; dall'Italia – from Italy; sulla tavola – on the table.

Essentials

First Things

Yes	Si
No	No
Please	Per favore/per piacere
Thank you	Grazie
No, thank you	No, grazie
Sorry	Mi scusi/mi dispiace

Language Problems

I'm English/American	Io sono inglese/americano
Do you speak English?	Parla inglese?
Does anyone here speak English?	C'è qualcuno qui che parla inglese?

I don't speak Italian	Io non parlo italiano
Do you understand (me)?	*(Mi) capisce?
I don't understand	Non capisco
Would you say that again, please?	Vuole ripetere, per favore?
Please speak slowly	Parli più lentamente, per favore
What does that mean?	Cosa vuol dire questo?
Can you translate this for me?	Me lo può tradurre?
Please write it down	Per cortesia, lo vuole scrivere?
What do you call this in Italian?	Come si chiama questo in italiano?
I will look it up in my phrase book	Guardo nel mio manuale di conversazione

Questions

Who?	Chi?
Where is/are .. ?	Dov'è/dove sono ... ?
When?	Quando?
Why?	Perché?
Where?	Dove?
What?	Cosa/che cosa?
How?	Come?

How much is/are . . . ?	Quanto costa/costano ?
How far	A che distanza è?
What's this ?	Cos'è questo ?
What do you want ?	Cosa desidera/cosa vuole ?
What must I do ?	Cosa debbo fare ?
What is the matter ?	Cosa c'é/cosa succede ?
Have you . . ./do you sell . . . ?	Ha . . ./vende . . . ?
Is there . . . ?	C'è . . . ?
Have you seen . . . ?	Ha visto . . . ?
May I have . . . ?	Posso avere . . . ?
I want/ should like . . .	Vorrei/ho bisogno di . . .
I don't want . . .	Non voglio . . .
Can you help me ?	Potrebbe aiutarmi ?
Can I help you ?	*Posso aiutarLa ?
Can you tell/give/show me . . . ?	Può dirmi/darmi/mostrarmi . . . ?

Useful statements

Here is/are . . .	Ecco . . .
I like it/them	Mi piace/mi piacciono
I don't like it/them	Non mi piace/piacciono
I know	Lo so

I don't know	Non lo so
I didn't know	Non lo sapevo
I think so	Credo di sì
I'm hungry/thirsty	Ho fame/sete
I'm tired	Sono stanco
I'm in a hurry	Ho fretta
I'm ready	Sono pronto
Leave me alone	Mi lasci in pace/mi lasci stare
Just a moment	*Mi scusi un momento
This way, please	*Da questa parte, per favore
Take a seat	*Si accomodi/si metta a sedere
Come in!	*Entri, prego/avanti, prego!
It's cheap	Costa poco/non è molto caro
It's too expensive	E molto caro/costa troppo
That's all	Nient'altro/questo è tutto
You're right	Lei ha ragione
You're wrong	Lei si sbaglia

Greetings

Good morning/good day	Buon giorno
Good afternoon	Buon giorno/buona sera
Good evening	Buona sera
Good night	Buona notte
Hallo	Ciao
How are you ?	Come sta ?
Very well, thank you	Molto bene, grazie
Good-bye	ArrivederLa/arrivederci/ciao
See you soon	A presto
See you tomorrow	A domani
Have a good journey	Buon viaggio
Good luck/all the best	Buona fortuna/i migliori auguri
Have a good time	Buon divertimento

Polite phrases

Sorry	Mi scusi/mi dispiace
Excuse me	Mi scusi
That's all right	Va benissimo
Not at all	Nient'affatto

Don't mention it (*after thanks*)	Prego
Don't worry	Non si preoccupi
It doesn't matter	Non importa/non fa niente
Is everything all right?	Tutto bene?
I beg your pardon?	Prego?
Am I disturbing you?	La disturbo?
I'm sorry to have troubled you	Mi scusi per il disturbo
Good/that's fine	Bene/va bene così

Opposites

before – after	prima – dopo
early – late	presto – tardi
first – last	primo – ultimo
now – later, then	ora – dopo, poi
far – near	lontano – vicino
here – there	qui – lì
in – out	dentro – fuori
inside – outside	dentro – fuori
under – over	sotto – sopra
big, large – small	grande, grande – piccolo
deep – shallow	profondo – basso

empty – full	vuoto – pieno
fat – lean	grasso – magro
heavy – light	pesante – leggero
high – low	alto – basso
long, tall – short	lungo, alto – breve, basso
narrow – wide	stretto – largo
thick – thin	spesso, grosso – sottile, fine
least – most	minimo – massimo
many – few	molti – pochi
more – less	più – meno
much – little	molto – poco
beautiful – ugly	bello – brutto
better – worse	meglio – peggio
cheap – dear	a buon mercato – costoso
clean – dirty	pulito – sporco
cold – hot, warm	freddo, fresco – caldo, tiepido
easy – difficult	facile – difficile
fresh – stale	fresco – stantio, andato a male
good – bad	buono – cattivo
new, young – old	nuovo, giovane – vecchio
nice – nasty	buono – cattivo, disgustoso
right – wrong	giusto – sbagliato
free – taken	libero – occupato
open – closed, shut	aperto – chiuso

quick – slow	rapido – lento
quiet – noisy	quieto, silenzioso – rumoroso
sharp – blunt	affilato – non taglia

Signs and public notices[1]

Acqua potabile	Drinking water
Acqua non potabile	Not for drinking
Affittasi	To let
Aperto	Open
Aperto dalle ore ... alle ore ...	Open from ... to ...
Ascensore	Lift/elevator
Attenzione	Caution
Banca	Bank
Bussare	Knock
Carabinieri	Police station
Chiuso	Closed
Divieto di entrata	No entry
Entrata	Entrance
Gabinetto	Lavatory/toilet

1. See also SIGNS TO LOOK FOR AT STATIONS (p. 39) and ROAD SIGNS (p. 51).

Gabinetto per signore/donne	Ladies
Gabinetto per signori/uomini	Gentlemen
Guida	Guide
Ingresso	Entrance
Ingresso libero	Admission free
Interprete	Interpreter
In vendita	For sale
I signori sono pregati di non . . .	You are requested not to . . .
I trasgressori verranno puniti a termini di legge	Trespassers will be prosecuted
Libero	Vacant/free/unoccupied
Occupato	Engaged/occupied
Pedoni	Pedestrians
Pericolo	Danger
Posto di Polizia	Police station
Posti in piedi	Standing room only
Privato	Private
Riservato	Reserved
Si prega di non . . .	Do not . . .
Spingere	Push
Stanza da affittare	Room to let
Suonare	Ring
Svendita	Sale
Tenere la destra	Keep right

Tirare	Pull
Tutto esaurito	House full (cinema, etc.)
Tutto occupato	No vacancies
Ufficio informazioni	Information
Ufficio postale	Post office
Uscita	Exit
Uscita di emergenza	Emergency exit
Vietato fumare	No smoking
Vietato l'ingresso	No admission

Money[1]

Is there an exchange bureau near here?	C'è un cambiavalute/ufficio cambi qui vicino?
Do you change travellers' cheques?	Può cambiare dei travellers' cheques?
Where can I change travellers' cheques?	Dove posso cambiare dei travellers' cheques?
Will you take a personal cheque?	Accetta assegni di conto corrente?
Do you have any identification?	*Ha un documento d'identità?
I want to change some pounds/dollars	Vorrei cambiare delle sterline/dei dollari
How much do I get for a pound/dollar?	A quanto cambia la sterlina/il dollaro?
What is the current rate of exchange?	Quanto è il cambio oggi?
Can you give me some small change?	Può darmi degli spiccioli?

1. In Italy, banks are open from 8.00 to 1.00, closed Saturday.

Sign here, please	*Vuol firmare qui, per favore
Go to the cashier	*Si accomodi alla cassa

Currency

Italian currency is the lira (plural lire).

Travel

On arrival

Passport control	*Controllo Passaporti
Your passport, please	*Passaporto, prego
Are you together ?	*I signori sono insieme ?
I'm travelling alone	Viaggio solo
I'm travelling with my wife/ a friend	Viaggio con mia moglie/un amico (un'amica)
I'm here on business/on holiday	Sono qui per affari/vengo in vacanza
What is your address in Italy/ Milan ?	*Quale è il suo indirizzo in Italia/ a Milano ?
How long are you staying here ?	*Quanto tempo rimane ?
How much money have you got ?	*Quanto denaro ha ?
I have . . . lire/pounds/dollars	Ho . . . lire/sterline/dollari
Customs	*Dogana

Goods/nothing to declare	Merci/niente da dichiarare
Which is your luggage ?	*Quali sono i suoi bagagli ?
Have you anything to declare ?	*Ha niente da dichiarare ?
I have a carton of cigarettes and a bottle of gin/wine	Ho una stecca di sigarette e una bottiglia di gin/vino
This is my luggage	Ecco i miei bagagli
Do you have any more luggage ?	*Ha altri bagagli ?
I have only my personal things in it	Ci sono solo effetti personali
Open this bag, please	*Apra questa valigia, per favore
Can I shut my case now ?	Posso chiudere la valigia ?
May I go ?	Posso andare ?
Where is the information bureau, please ?	Dov'è l'Ufficio Informazioni, per favore ?
Porter	Facchino/portabagagli
Would you take these bags to a taxi/the bus ?	Vuol portare questi bagagli al tassì/all'autobus ?
What's the price for each piece of luggage ?	Quanto costa a collo ?
I shall take this myself	Questa la porto io
That's not mine	Questa non è mia
Would you call a taxi ?	Mi può chiamare un tassì, per favore ?
How much do I owe you ?	Quanto Le devo ?

Signs to look for at stations, etc.

Arrivals	Arrivi
Booking office	Prenotazioni
Buses	Autobus/pullman
Connections	Coincidenze
Departures	Partenze
Exchange	Cambio/cambiavalute
Gentlemen	Signori/gabinetti/toilette
Information	Informazioni
Ladies' room	Signore/gabinetti per signora
Left luggage	Deposito bagagli
Lost property	Oggetti smarriti
Main lines	Linee principali
Non-smoker	Vietato fumare
Refreshments	Rinfreschi/ristoratore
Reservations	Prenotazioni
Smoker	Fumatori
Suburban lines	Linee locali
Taxis	Tassì
Tickets	Biglietti
Underground	Metropolitana
Waiting room	Sala d'aspetto

Buying a ticket

Where is the tourist office ?	Dov'è l'ufficio turistico
Where's the nearest travel agency?	Dov'è agenzia di viaggi la più vicina?
Have you a timetable, please ?	Ha un orario, per favore ?
What's the tourist return fare to . . . ?	Quanto costa un biglietto turistico di andata e ritorno per . . . ?
How much is it first class to . . . ?	Quanto costa un biglietto di prima classe per . . . ?
A second class single to . . .	Un biglietto di seconda classe, solo andata, per . . .
A single ticket to . . .	Un biglietto di sola andata per . . .
A return ticket to . . .	Un biglietto di andata e ritorno per . . .
A day return to . . .	Un biglietto a riduzione per . . .
Is there a special rate for children ?	C'è uno sconto per i ragazzi ?
How old is he (she)/are they ?	*Quanti anni ha/hanno ?
How long is this ticket valid ?	Per quanti giorni è valido questo biglietto ?
A book of tickets, please	Un mazzetto di biglietti, per favore
Is there a supplementary charge ?	C'è da pagare un supplemento ?

By train and underground[1]

RESERVATIONS AND INQUIRIES

Where's the railway station?	Dov'è la stazione?
Where is the ticket office?	Dov'è la biglietteria?
Two seats on the 11.15 tomorrow to ...	Due posti sul treno delle undici e quindici di domani per ...
I want to reserve a sleeper	Vorrei riservare un posto in vagone letto
How much does a couchette cost?	Quanto costa una cuccetta?
I want to register this luggage through to ...	Vorrei spedire questi bagagli raccomandati a ...
Is it an express or a local train?[2]	E un treno diretto o accelerato?
Is there an earlier/later train?	Ci sono altri treni prima di questo/dopo questo?
Is there a restaurant car on the train?	C'è un vagone ristorante su questo treno?

1. For help in understanding the answers to these and similar questions see TIME (p. 145), NUMBERS (p. 151), DIRECTIONS (p. 48).

2. Trains are classified as follows: *Rapido* – fast trains running between main towns, sometimes only first class. A supplement is charged (about 25 per cent of normal single fare). *Direttissimo* – long distance express trains, first and second class. *Diretto* – express trains, first and second class. *Accelerato* – local trains. Luggage can often be transported for the whole journey in the luggage car, and this service is called *bagaglio a seguito passeggero*. Certain Trans-European Express trains go through Italy. They are only first class and a supplement must be paid.

CHANGING

Is there a through train to . . . ?	C'è un treno diretto per . . . ?
Do I have to change ?	Debbo cambiare ?
Where do I change ?	Dove debbo cambiare ?
What time is there a connection to . . . ?	A che ora c'è la coincidenza per . . . ?

DEPARTURE

When does the train leave ?	A che ora parte questo treno ?
Which platform does the train to . . . leave from ?	Da quale binario parte il treno per . . . ?
Is this the train for . . . ?	E questo il treno per . . . ?

ARRIVAL

When does it get to . . . ?	A che ora arriva a . . . ?
Does the train stop at . . . ?	Ferma a . . . questo treno ?
How long do we stop here ?	Quanto ci fermiamo qui ?
Is the train late ?	E in ritardo questo treno ?
When does the train from . . . get in ?	A che ora arriva il treno da . . . ?
At which platform ?	Su quale binario ?

ON THE TRAIN

We have reserved seats	Abbiamo posti riservati
Is this seat free ?	E libero questo posto ?
This seat is taken	Questo posto è occupato
Conductor	Capotreno

By air

Where's the Alitalia office ?	Dov'è l'ufficio dell'Alitalia ?
I'd like to book two seats on Monday's plane to . . .	Vorrei prenotare due posti sull'aereo di lunedì per . . .
Is there a flight to Milan next Thursday ?	Ci sono servizi aerei per Milano giovedì prossimo ?
What is the flight number ?	Qual'è il numero di volo ?
When does it leave/arrive ?	A che ora parte/arriva ?
When does the next plane leave ?	A che ora parte il prossimo aereo ?
Is there a bus to the airport/to the town ?	C'è un autobus per l'aeroporto/ per andare in città ?
When must I check in ?	A che ora c'è il controllo ?
Please cancel my reservation to . . .	Vorrei disdire la mia prenotazione per . . .
I'd like to change my reservation to . . .	Vorrei cambiare la mia prenotazione per . . .

By ship

Is there a boat from here to . . .?	C'è un servizio marittimo per . . .?
How long does it take to get to . . .?	Quanto tempo mette per arrivare a . . .?
How often do the boats leave?	Ogni quanto partono i battelli?
Where does the boat put in?	Dove fa scalo questo battello?
Does it call at . . .?	Si ferma a . . .?
When does the next boat leave?	Quando parte il prossimo battello?
Can I book a single berth cabin?	Posso riservare una cabina ad un letto?
How many berths are there in this cabin?	Quante cuccette ci sono in questa cabina?
When must we go on board?	A che ora dobbiamo essere a bordo?
When do we dock?	A che ora arriviamo in porto?
How long do we stay in port?	Quanto rimaniamo in porto?
(Car) ferry	Traghetto

By bus or coach

Where's the bus station?	Dov'è la stazione degli autobus?
Where's the coach station?	Dov'è la stazione dei pullman?
Bus stop	Fermata dell'autobus
Request stop	Fermata a richiesta
When does the coach leave?	Quando parte il pullman?
What time do we get to . . . ?	A che ora arriviamo a . . . ?
What stops does it make?	In quali posti si ferma?
Is it a long journey?	E un viaggio molto lungo?
We want to take a sightseeing tour round the city	Vogliamo fare un giro turistico della città
Is there an organized tour of the town?	Ci sono giri organizzati della città?
What is the fare?	Quanto costa?
Does the bus/coach call at our hotel?	Questo autobus/pullman passa dal nostro albergo?
Is there an excursion to . . . tomorrow?	C'è una gita a . . . domani?
What time is the next bus?	A che ora c'è il prossimo autobus?
How often does the . . . run?	Ogni quanto passa l'autobus . . . ?
Has the last bus gone?	E già partito l'ultimo autobus?
Does this bus go to the centre?	Passa dal centro questo autobus?
Does it go to the beach?	Passa vicino alla spiaggia?

Does this bus go to the station?	Va alla stazione questo autobus?
Does it go near . . .?	Passa vicino a . . .?
Where can I get a bus to . . .?	Dove posso prendere un autobus per . . .?
Which bus goes to . . .?	Quale autobus va a . . .?
I want to go to . . .	Io voglio andare a . . .
Where do I get off?	Dove debbo scendere?
The bus to . . . stops over there	*L'autobus per . . . ferma là
A number . . . goes to . . .	*Il numero . . . va a . . .
You must take a number . . .	*Lei deve prendere il numero . . .
You get off at the next stop	*Scenda alla prossima fermata
The buses run every ten minutes/every hour	*C'è un autobus ogni dieci minuti/ogni ora

By taxi

Please get me a taxi	Vuol chiamarmi un tassì, per favore?
Where can I get a taxi?	Dove posso prendere un tassì?
Are you free?	E libero?
Please take me to Hotel Central/ the station/this address	Mi vuol portare all'Hotel Centrale/alla stazione/a questo indirizzo

Can you hurry, I'm late?	Può andare un po' più in fretta, sono in ritardo ?
I want to go through the centre	Vorrei passare dal centro
Please wait a minute	Aspetti un momento, per favore
Stop here	Fermi qui
Is it far?	E molto lontano?
How much do you charge by the hour/for the day?	Quanto prende all'ora/ a giornata ?
I'd like to go to . . . How much would you charge?	Vorrei andare a . . . Quanto costa ?
How much is it?	Quanto è?
That's too much	E troppo
I am not prepared to spend that much	No, grazie, è più di quanto posso spendere
It's a lot, but all right	E un po'caro, ma va bene

Directions

Excuse me – could you tell me the way to . . .?	Mi scusi, può indicarmi la strada per . . .?
Where is . . .?	Dov'è . . .?
Is this the way to . . .?	E questa la strada per . . .?
Which is the road for . . .?	Quale è la strada per . . .?
How far is it to . . .?	Quanto c'è di qui a . . .?
How many kilometres?	Quanti chilometri?
We want to get on to the motorway to . . .	Vorremmo prendere l'autostrada per . . .
Which is the best road to . . .?	Quale è la migliore strada per . . .?
Where does this road lead to?	Dove porta questa strada?
Is it a good road?	E una strada in buone condizioni?
Is it a motorway?	E un'autostrada?
Is there any danger of avalanches?	C'è pericolo di valanghe?

Will we get to . . . by evening?	Arriveremo a . . . prima di sera?
Where are we now?	Dove siamo adesso?
What is the name of this place?	Come si chiama questo posto?
Please show me on the map	Può farmi vedere sulla mappa, per favore
It's that way	*È in questa direzione/di qui
It isn't far	*Non è lontano di qui
Follow this road for . . . kilometres	*Segua questa strada per . . . chilometri
Keep straight on	*Continui a diritto
Turn right at the crossroads	*Al crocevia volti a destra
Take the second road on the left	*Prenda la seconda strada a sinistra
Turn right at the traffic-lights	*Quando è al semaforo, volti a destra
Turn left after the bridge	*Dopo il ponte giri a sinistra
The best road is . . .	*La migliore strada è . . .
Take this road as far as . . . and ask again	*Segua questa strada fino a . . . e chieda di nuovo

Motoring

General

Have you a road map, please?	Ha una carta stradale, per favore?
Where is a car park?	Dov'è un parcheggio?
(How long) can I park here?	(Quanto tempo) si può parcare qui?
How long can I park here?	Si può tenere la macchina qui?
No parking	*Divieto di parcheggio/ parcheggio vietato
Is this your car?	E Sua questa macchina?
May I see your licence, please?	*Posso vedere la Sua patente, per favore?
How far is the next petrol station?	A che distanza è il più vicino distributore (di benzina)?

Car Hire

Where can I hire a car?	Dove posso noleggiare una macchina?
I want to hire a car and a driver/a self drive car	Vorrei noleggiare una macchina con autista/vorrei prendere a nolo una macchina
How much is it by the hour/day/week?	Quanto costa l'ora/a giornata/per settimana?
I need a car for two days/a week	Ho bisogno di una macchina per due giorni/una settimana
Does that include mileage?	Il chilometraggio è compreso?
The charge per kilometre is . . .	*La tariffa è di Lire . . . a chilometro
What kind of insurance do you want?	Che tipo di assicurazione vuole?

Road Signs

Cautela	Caution
Curve	Winding road
Diversione	Diversion
Disco blu	Parking disc required
Dogana	Customs

Fermata	Stop
Lavori in corso	Road works ahead
Limite di velocità	Speed limit
Parcheggio vietato	No parking
Passaggio a livello	Level crossing
Pericolo	Danger
Prudenza	Attention/caution
Rallentare	Slow
Salita rapida	Steep hill
Semaforo	Traffic lights
Senso unico	One way (street)
Senso vietato	No entry
Sosta autorizzata	Parking allowed
Strada interrotta	Road blocked
Superficie irregolare/ sdrucciolevole	Uneven/slippery surface
Svolte/curve	Bends/curves
Tenere la destra	Keep right
Tenersi in corsia	Keep in lane
Usare i fanali	Lights on/use headlights
Uscita autoveicoli	Exit for lorries

At the garage or petrol station

Where is the nearest petrol station?	Dov'è il distributore più vicino?
How far is the next petrol station?	A che distanza è il distributore più vicino?
... litres of petrol, and please check the oil and water	... litri di benzina, e per favore controlli l'olio e l'acqua
Fill it up	Faccia il pieno
How much is petrol a litre?	Quanto costa un litro di benzina?
... lire worth of petrol, please	... lire di benzina, per favore
The oil needs changing	Bisognerebbe cambiare l'olio
Check the tyre pressure, please	Controlli le gomme, per favore
Please change the tyre	Vuol cambiare la gomma, per favore
Could you check the brakes/transmission fluid?	Può controllare i freni/il giunto idraulico?
Would you clean the windscreen, please?	Può pulirmi il parabrezza, per favore?
Please wash the car	Vuol lavare la macchina, per favore
Can I garage the car here?	Posso lasciare la macchina in questo garage?
What time does the garage close?	A che ora chiude il garage?
Where are the toilets?	Dove sono le toilette?

Repairs

My car's broken down	Ho un guasto alla macchina
Can I use your phone?	Posso usare il telefono?
Where is there a . . . agency?	Dov'è l'Agenzia della . . .?
Have you a breakdown service?	Ha un servizio riparazioni?
Is there a mechanic?	C'è un meccanico?
Can you send someone to repair it/ tow it away?	Può mandare qualcuno a ripararla/rimorchiarla?
It is an automatic and cannot be towed	È automatica, e non si può rimorchiare
Where is your car?	*Dov'è la macchina?
Where are you now?	*Dove si trova Lei adesso?
I am on the road from . . . to . . . near kilometre post . . .	Sono sulla strada da . . . a . . . vicino al chilometro . . .
How long will you be?	Fra quanto tempo sarà qui?
I want the car serviced	Vorrei far revisionare l'automobile
The battery is flat, it needs charging	La batteria è scarica, ha bisogno di essere caricata
This tyre is flat/punctured	Questa gomma è sgonfia/forata
The valve is leaking	Questa valvola perde
The radiator is leaking	Il radiatore perde acqua
My car won't start	La mia macchina non parte
It's not running properly	Procede a scosse

The engine is overheating	Il motore riscalda troppo
I've got electrical trouble	Deve esserci un guasto nel sistema elettrico
The lock is broken/jammed	La serratura è rotta/bloccata
The engine is firing badly	L'accensione è difettosa
The engine knocks	Il motore batte in testa
Can you change this plug?	Può cambiare questa candela?
There's a petrol/oil leak	C'è una perdita di benzina/d'olio
There's a smell of petrol/rubber	Si sente odore di benzina/di gomma
Something is wrong with my car/the engine/the lights/the clutch/the gearbox/the brakes/the steering	Ho un guasto alla macchina/nel motore/ai fanali/nella frizione/nella scatola del cambio/ai freni/allo sterzo
The carburettor needs adjusting	Il carburatore deve essere regolato
Can you repair it?	Può ripararla?
How long will it take to repair?	Quanto tempo ci vuole per ripararla?
What will it cost?	Quanto mi verrà a costare?
When can I pick the car up?	Quando posso venire a prendere la macchina?
I need it as soon as possible	Ne ho bisogno il più presto possibile

I need it in three hours/ tomorrow morning	Ne avrei bisogno fra tre ore/ domani mattina
It will take two days	*Ci vorranno due giorni
We can repair it temporarily	*La possiamo riparare provvisoriamente
We haven't the right spares	*Non abbiamo i pezzi di ricambio
We have to send for the spares	*Dobbiamo far venire i pezzi di ricambio
You will need a new ...	*Ci vuole un nuovo m/una nuova f ...
Could I have an itemized bill, please?	Può farmi il conto articolo per articolo, per favore?

Parts of a car

accelerate (to)	accelerare	a-che-le-ra-ray
accelerator	l'acceleratore m	a-che-le-ra-to-ray
alternator	l'alternatore m	al-ter-na-tor-ay
anti-freeze	l'anticongelante m	an-tee-kon-je-lan-tay
axle	l'asse m	as-say
battery	la batteria	bat-tair-ee-a
bonnet	il cofano	ko-fa-no
boot/trunk	il portabagagli	por-ta-ba-ga-lee

brake	il freno	fre-no
breakdown	il guasto	gwas-toh
bulb	la lampadina	lam-pa-dee-na
bumper	il paraurti	pa-ra-oor-tee
carburettor	il carburatore	kar-boo-ra-to-ray
choke	la presa d'aria	pray-za da-rya
crankshaft	la manovella	ma-no-vel-la
cylinder	il cilindro	chee-leen-droh
differential gear	il differenziale	deef-fer-en-tsee-a-lay
dip stick	la coppa dell'olio	kop-pa del lol-yoh
distilled water	l'acqua distillata *f*	ak-wa dee-steel-la-ta
distributor	il distributore	dee-stree-boo-to-ray
door	lo sportello/la portiera	spor-tel-lo/ por-tyair-a
doorhandle	la maniglia dello sportello	ma-nee-lya del-lo spor-tel-lo
drive (to)	guidare	gwee-da-ray
driver	l'autista *m*	ow-tees-ta
dynamo	la dinamo	dee-na-mo
engine	il motore	mo-to-ray
exhaust	lo scappamento	skap-pa-men-toh
fan	il ventilatore	ven-tee-la-to-ray
fanbelt	la cinghia del ventilatore	cheen-ghee-a del ven-tee-la-to-ray

(oil) filter	il filtro (dell'olio)	feel-troh (del lol-yoh)
flat tyre	la gomma sgonfia	gom-ma sgon-fee-a
foglamp	il fanale antinebbia	fan-al-ay an-tee-neb-bya
fusebox	la valvola	val-vo-la
gasket	la guarnizione	gwar-need-zyo-nay
gear	la marcia/ la velocità	mar-chya/ve-lo-chee-ta
gear box	la scatola del cambio	ska-to-la del kam-byo
gear lever	la leva del cambio	le-va del kam-byo
grease (to)	ingrassare	een-gras-sa-ray
handbrake	il freno a mano	fre-no a ma-no
heater	il riscaldamento	rees-kal-da-men-toh
horn	il clacson	klak-son
ignition	l'accensione *f*	a-chen-see-o-nay
ignition key	la chiavetta dell'accensione	kya-vet-ta del-a-chen-see-o-nay
indicator	l'indicatore *m*/ la freccia	een-dee-ka-to-ray/ fre-chya
jack	il martinetto/il cricco	mar-tee-net-toh/ kreck-koh
lights – head/rear	i fanali anteriori i fanali posteriori	fa-na-lee an-te-ree-or-ee pos-te-ree-or-ee
side	i fanali di posizione	dee po-zit-see-o-nay
lock/catch	la serratura	ser-ra-too-ra
mirror	lo specchietto	spek-kyet-toh

number plate	la targa	tar-ga
nut	il dado	da-doh
oil	l'olio *m*	ol-yoh
petrol	la benzina	ben-zee-na
petrol can	il bidone di benzina	bee-do-nay dee ben-zee-na
piston	il pistone	pees-to-nay
plug	la candela	kan-de-la
propeller shaft	l'albero di trasmissione *m*	ál-be-ro dee tras-mees-syo-nay
pump	la pompa	pom-pa
radiator	il radiatore	ra-dee-a-to-ray
rear axle	il ponte posteriore	pon-tay pos-te-ree-or-e
reverse (to)	fare marcia indietro	fa-ray mar-chya een-dye-troh
reverse	la retromarcia	re-tro-mar-chya
seat	il sedile	say-dee-lay
shock absorber	l'ammortizzatore *m*	am-mor-teed-za-to-ray
silencer	il silenziatore	see-len-tsya-to-ray
spanner	la chiave inglese	kee-a-vay eeng-lay-zay
spare tyre	la gomma di scorta	gom-ma dee skor-ta
spares	i pezzi di ricambio	ped-zee dee ree-kam-byo
sparking plug	la candela	kan-de-la

speed	la velocità	ve-lo-chee-tà
speedometer	il tachimetro	ta-kee-me-troh
spring	la molla	mol-la
stall (to)	fermarsi a scosse	fer-mar-see a skos-say
starter	il motorino d'avviamento	mo-to-ree-no dav-vya-men-toh
steering	lo sterzo	ster-tso
steering wheel	il volante	vo-lan-tay
suspension	la sospensione	sos-pen-see-o-nay
tank	il serbatoio	ser-ba-toy-oh
tappets	le punterie	poon-ter-ee-ay
transmission	la trasmissione	tras-mees-syo-nay
tyre pressure	le pressione delle gomme	pres-syo-nay del-lay gom-may
tyres	i copertoni/le gomme	ko-per-to-nee/ gom-may
valve	la válvola	val-vo-la
wheel	la ruota	rwo-ta
window	il vetro	ve-troh
windscreen	il parabrezza	pa-ra-bred-za
windscreen washers	gli spruzzatori	sproot-za-to-ree
windscreen wipers	i tergicristalli	ter-jee-krees-tal-lee

Accommodation

Booking a room

Rooms to let/vacancies	*Affittasi/camere da affittare
No vacancies	*Tutto occupato
Have you a room for the night?	Ha una camera per stanotte?
I've reserved a room; my name is ...	Ho riservato una camera. Mi chiamo ...
Do you know another hotel?	Può indicarmi un altro albergo?
I want a single room with a shower	Vorrei una camera ad un letto con doccia
We want a room with a double bed and a bathroom	Vorremmo una camera matrimoniale con bagno
Have you a room with twin beds?	Ha una camera con due letti?
How long will you be staying?	*Quanto tempo rimane (rimangono *pl*)?

Is it for one night only?	*Rimane (rimangono *pl*) solo una notte?
I want a room for two or three days/a week/until Friday	Vorrei una camera per due o tre giorni/per una settimana/fino a venerdì
What floor is the room on?	A che piano è questa camera?
Is there a lift/elevator?	C'è l'ascensore?
Have you a room on the first floor?	Ha una camera al primo piano?
May I see the room?	Posso vedere la camera?
I like this room, I'll take it	Questa camera mi piace, la prendo
I don't like this room	Questa camera non mi piace molto
Have you another one?	Ne ha un'altra?
I want a quiet room	Vorrei una camera molto tranquilla
There's too much noise	C'è troppo rumore
I'd like a room with a balcony	Vorrei una camera con balcone
Have you a room looking on to the street/sea?	Ha una camera che dà sulla strada/sul lungomare?
Is there a telephone/radio/television in the room?	C'è il telefono/la radio/la televisione in questa stanza?
We've only a double room	*Abbiamo solo una camera matrimoniale
This is the only room vacant	*Questa è l'unica camera libera

We shall have another room tomorrow	*Avremo un altra camera libera domani
The room is only available tonight	*Possiamo darLe questa camera solo per stanotte
How much is the room per night?	Quanto costa questa camera per notte?
Have you nothing cheaper?	Non ha niente di meno costoso?
What do we pay for the children?	I ragazzi, quanto pagano?
Could you put a cot in the room, please?	Può mettere una culla, per piacere?
Are service and tax included?	Il servizio e le tasse sono comprese nel prezzo?
How much is the room without meals?	Quanto è la camera senza i pasti?
How much is full board/half board?	Quanto è la pensione completa/ la mezza pensione?
Is breakfast included in the price?	La prima colazione è compresa nel prezzo?
Do you have a weekly rate?	Fa dei prezzi settimanali?
Please fill in the registration form	*Vuol compilare la scheda di registrazione, per cortesia?
Could you leave your passport, please?	*Vuol lasciare il passaporto, per favore?

In your room

Room service	Servizio di camera
Could we have breakfast in our room	Potremmo avere la prima colazione in camera?
Please wake me at 8.30	Mi può svegliare alle otto e mezza, per favore
There's no ashtray in my room	Non ci sono portaceneri in camera mia
Can I have more hangers, please?	Posso avere qualche altra gruccia?
Is there a point for an electric razor?	C'è una presa per rasoio elettrico?
What's the voltage?	Che voltaggio ha?
Where is the bathroom/the lavatory?	Dov'è il bagno/il gabinetto?
Is there a shower?	C'è la doccia?
There are no towels in my room	In camera mia non ci sono asciugamani
There's no soap	Non c'è sapone
There's no (hot) water	Non c'è acqua (calda)
There's no plug in my washbasin	Nel mio lavandino non c'è tappo
There's no toilet paper in the lavatory	Nel gabinetto non c'è carta igienica
The lavatory won't flush	Lo sciacquone non funzione

May I have the key to the bathroom, please?	Posso avere la chiave del bagno, per favore?
May I have another blanket/ another pillow?	Posso avere un'altra coperta/ un altro cuscino?
These sheets are dirty	Queste lenzuola sono sporche
I can't open my window, please open it	Non posso aprire la finestra. Vuole aprirla Lei, per favore?
It's too hot/cold	Fa troppo caldo/freddo
Can the heating be turned up/ turned down/turned off?	Può aprire/abbassare/chiudere il riscaldamento?
Is the room air-conditioned?	Questa camera è ad aria condizionata?
The air conditioning doesn't work	Il condizionamento aria non funziona
Come in!	Entri/avanti!
Put it on the table, please	Lo metta sulla tavola, per favore
Would you clean these shoes, please?	Mi può lucidare le scarpe, per favore?
Would you clean this dress, please?	Mi può pulire questo abito, per favore?
Would you press this suit, please?	Mi può stirare questo abito, per favore?
When will it be ready?	Quando sarà pronto?
It will be ready tomorrow	*Sarà pronto domani

At the porter's desk

My key, please	La chiave, per favore
Can you keep this in your safe?	Può tenere questo nella cassaforte?
Are there any letters for me?	C'è posta per me?
Are there any messages for me?	Ci sono messaggi per me?
If anyone phones, tell them I'll be back at 4.30	Se qualcuno telefona, dica che sarò di ritorno alle quattro e mezza
No one telephoned	*Non ci sono state telefonate per Lei
There's a lady/gentleman to see you	*C'è una signora/un signore che desidera vederLa
Please ask her/him to come up	Le/gli dica di salire, per favore
I'm coming down	Scendo subito
Have you any writing paper/envelopes/stamps?	Ha della carta da lettere/delle buste/dei francobolli?
Please send the chambermaid/the waiter	Può mandare la cameriera/il cameriere, per favore
I need a guide/an interpreter	Vorrei una guida/un interprete
Where is the dining room?	Dov'è il ristorante?
What time is breakfast/lunch/dinner?	A che ora è la prima colazione/la colazione/la cena?
Is there a garage?	C'è un garage?

Is the hotel open all night?

Rimane aperto tutta la notte
questo albergo?

What time does it close?

A che ora chiude?

Departure

I have to leave tomorrow

Debbo partire domani

Can you make up my bill?

Può prepararmi il conto?

I shall be coming back on . . .;
can I book a room for that date?

Ritornerò il . . .; può riservarmi
una camera per questa data?

Could you have my luggage
brought down?

Può far portare giù i bagagli?

Please call a taxi for me

Per favore, vuol chiamare un
tassì

Thank you for a pleasant stay

Grazie di tutto. E stato un
soggiorno molto piacevole

Meeting people

How are you?	Come sta (state *pl*)
Fine, thank you; and you?	Bene, grazie; e Lei?
What is your name?	Come si chiama?
May I introduce myself?	Posso presentarmi?
My name is ...	Mi chiamo ...
This is ...	Questo/questa è ...
Have you met ...?	Conosce ...?
Glad to meet you	Lieto di conoscerLa
What lovely/awful weather	Che bel/brutto tempo
Isn't it cold/hot today?	Non è piuttosto freddo/caldo oggi?
Do you think it's going to rain/snow?	Pensa che pioverà/nevicherà?
Will it be fine tomorrow?	Sarà una bella giornata domani?
Am I disturbing you?	La disturbo?
Go away	Se ne vada

Leave me alone	Mi lasci in pace
Sorry to have troubled you	Mi scusi per il disturbo
Are you on holiday?	È qui in vacanza?
Is this your first time here?	È la prima volta che Lei è qui?
Do you like it here?	Le piace da queste parti?
Are you on your own?	È solo/sola?
I am with my family/parents/ a friend	Sono qui con la famiglia/ i genitori/un amico *m*/una amica *f*
Which part of Italy do you come from?	Da che parte d'Italia viene?
I come from . . .	Vengo da . . ./Sono di . . .
What do you do?	Quale è la sua occupazione?
What are you studying?	Cosa studia?
I'm on holiday/a business trip	Sono in vacanza/in giro d'affari
Would you like a cigarette?	Posso offrirLe una sigaretta?
Try one of mine	Ne provi una delle mie
They are very mild/rather strong	Sono leggere/piuttosto forti
Do you have a light, please?	Ha un fiammifero, per favore?
Do you smoke?	Lei fuma?
No, I don't, thanks	No, non fumo, grazie
Help yourself	Si serva
Can I get you a drink/another drink?	Posso offrirLe qualcosa da bere/ qualcos'altro da bere?
I'd like a . . . please	Prenderei volentieri un . . .

Going out

Are you waiting for someone?	Aspetta qualcuno?
Are you doing anything tonight/ tomorrow afternoon?	Ha già dei programmi per stasera/domani pomeriggio?
Could we have coffee/a drink together?	Potremmo prendere un caffè/ bere qualcosa insieme?
Could we go out together?	Possiamo uscire insieme?
Shall we go to the cinema/ theatre/beach?	Vogliamo andare al cinema/a teatro/al mare?
Would you like to go dancing?	Vuole andare a ballare?
Would you like to go for a drive?	Vuole fare un giro in macchina?
Do you know a good disco/ restaurant?	Conosce una buona discoteca/ un buon ristorante?
Can you come to dinner?	Può venire a cena?
We are giving a party, would you like to come?	Noi diamo un ricevimento, vuol venire?
Can I bring a (girl) friend?	Posso portare anche un amico m/ una amica f?
Thank you for the invitation	Grazie dell'invito
Where shall we meet?	Dove ci troviamo?
What time shall I/we come?	A che ora debbo/debbiamo venire?
Could you meet me at . . . ?	Possiamo trovarci a . . . ?
What time do you have to be back?	A che ora deve essere di ritorno?

May I see you home?	Posso accompagnarLa a casa?
Can we give you a lift home/to your hotel?	Possiamo darLe un passaggio fino a casa/fino all'albergo?
Can we meet again?	Possiamo vederci di nuovo?
Where do you live?	Dove abita?
Would you give me your telephone number?	Vuol darmi il Suo numero di telefono?
Do you live alone?	Vive solo/sola?
Thank you for the pleasant evening	Grazie per la bellissima serata
I hope to see you again soon	Spero di rivederLa presto
See you soon/later/tomorrow	A presto/a più tardi/a domani

Restaurant

Going to a restaurant

Can you suggest a good restaurant/a cheap restaurant/a vegetarian restaurant?

Mi può indicare un buon ristorante/un ristorante a buon mercato/un ristorante vegetariano?

I'd like to book a table for four at 1 p.m.

Vorrei riservare un tavolo per quattro persone per l'una

I've reserved a table; my name is ...

Ho riservato un tavolo, sono ...

We did not make a reservation

Non abbiamo riservato un tavolo

Is there a table free on the terrace/by the window/in a corner?

Ha un tavolo sulla veranda/vicino alla finestra/in un angolo?

Have you a table for three?

Ha un tavolo per tre?

This way, please

*Da questa parte, per favore

You would have to wait about . . . minutes	*Dovrebbe aspettare circa . . . minuti
We shall have a table free in half an hour	*Avremo un tavolo libero tra mezz'ora
We don't serve lunch until 12.30	*Cominciamo a servire il pranzo alle dodici e mezzo
We don't serve dinner until 8 p.m.	*Cominciamo a servire la cena alle otto
We stop serving at 11 o'clock	*Smettiamo di servire alle undici
Where is the cloakroom?	Dov'è la toilette?
It is downstairs/upstairs	*E al piano di sotto/al piano di sopra

Ordering

Service and V.A.T. (not) included	*Servizio e I.V.A. (non) sono compresi
Cover charge	*Coperto
Waiter/waitress	Cameriere/cameriera
May I see the menu/the wine list, please?	Posso vedere il menu/la lista dei vini, per favore?
Is there a set menu for lunch?	Ha un pranzo a prezzo fisso?
We are in a hurry	Abbiamo fretta
Do you serve snacks?	Si può fare uno spuntino?

I want something light	Vorrei qualcosa di leggere
Could we have a small helping?	Potremmo avere una mezza porzione?
What is the dish of the day?	Cos'è il piatto del giorno?
What do you recommend?	Cosa raccomanda Lei?
Can you tell me what this is?	Mi può dire che cos'è questo piatto?
What are the specialities of the restaurant/of the region?	Quali sono le specialità di questo ristorante/di questa regione?
Would you like to try ...?	*Vuol provare ...?
There's no more ...	*Non abbiamo più ...
I'd like ...	Vorrei ...
May I have peas instead of beans?	Posso avere piselli invece di fagioli?
Is it hot or cold?	È un piatto caldo o freddo?
Where are our drinks?	Non ci ha ancora portato da bere
Why does it take so long?	Perchè bisogna aspettare così tanto?
This isn't what I ordered, I want ...	Non ho ordinato questo, io voglio ...
I don't want any oil/sauce with it	Lo voglio senza olio/senza salsa
Some more bread, please	Vorremmo ancora del pane, per favore
A little more, please	Un po' di più, per favore

That's enough, thank you	Basta così, grazie
This is bad/uncooked/stale	Questo è cattivo/poco cotto/ andato a male
This is cold/too salty/ overcooked	Questo è freddo/troppo salato/ stracotto
This plate/knife/spoon/glass is not clean	Questo piatto/coltello/ cucchiaio/bicchiere è sporco

Paying

The bill, please	Il conto, prego
Does it include service?	Il servizio è compreso?
Please check the bill – I don't think it's correct	Vuol controllare il conto. Non mi sembra esatto
I didn't have soup	Non ho preso la minestra
I had chicken, not steak	Ho preso pollo, non bistecca
May we have separate bills?	Ci faccia il conto separato
Keep the change	Tenga il resto

Breakfast and tea

Breakfast	La prima colazione
What time is breakfast served?	A che ora servono la prima colazione?
A large white coffee, please	Un cappuccino, per favore
A black espresso coffee	Un caffè nero/espresso
A cup of tea, please	Una tazza di tè, per favore
I'd like tea with milk/lemon	Vorrei tè con latte/al limone
May we have some sugar, please?	Lo zucchero, per favore
A roll and butter	Un panino con burro
Toast	Un toast
We'd like more butter, please	Vorremmo ancora del burro, per favore
Have you some jam/marmalade?	Ha della marmellata/marmellata d'aranci?
A hard-boiled/soft-boiled egg	Un uovo sodo/à la coque
Bacon and eggs, please	Uova e pancetta, per favore
Ham	Il prosciutto cotto
What fruit juices have you?	Che succhi di frutta ha?
Orange/grapefruit/tomato juice	Un succo d'arancio/di pompelmo/di pomodoro
A cup of chocolate	Una tazza di cioccolata
Yogurt	Yogurt

Snacks and picnics 77

Snacks and picnics

Can I have a . . . sandwich, please?	Mi dà un sandwich di . . ., per favore?
What are those things over there?	Cos' è questo?
What are they made of?	Di cosa son fatti?
What is in them?	Cosa c'è dentro?
I'll have one of these, please	Me ne dia uno, per favore
Biscuits	Biscotti
Bread	Pane
Butter	Burro
Cheese	Formaggio
Chips	Patatine fritte
Chocolate bar	Tavoletta di cioccolata
Egg/eggs	Uovo/uova
Ham	Prosciutto
Ice-cream	Gelato
Pancakes	Frittelle
Pickles	Sottaceti
Meat/fruit pie	Pasticcio di carne/di frutta
Roll	Panino
Salad	Insalata
Sausage	Salsiccia
Snack	Spuntino

Snack bar	Tavola calda
Soup	Minestra
Tomato	Pomodori
Waffles	Cialde

Drinks[1]

What will you have to drink?	*Cosa desidera bere?
A bottle of the local wine, please	Una bottiglia di vino locale, per favore
Do you serve wine by the glass?	Vende vino a bicchieri?
Carafe/glass	Una carafa/un bicchiere
Bottle/half bottle	Una bottiglia/una mezza bottiglia
Two glasses of beer, please	Due birre, per favore
Do you have draught beer?	Ha birra alla spina?
Two more beers	Altre due birre
Large/small beer	Una birra grande/piccola
Neat	Liscio
On the rocks	Con ghiaccio
With soda water	. . . e soda
With water	. . . e acqua

1. For the names of beverages see p. 93.

Mineral water (with/without gas)	Acqua minerale (gassata/non gassata)
I'd like another glass of water, please	Vorrei un altro bicchiere d'acqua, per favore
The same again, please	Lo stesso, per favore
Three black coffees and one with cream	Tre caffè neri e uno con panna
May we have an ashtray?	Possiamo avere un portacenere?

Restaurant vocabulary

ashtray	il portacenere
bill	il conto
bowl	la scodella
cigarettes	le sigarette
cloakroom	il guardaroba
course (dish)	la portata/il piatto
cup	la tazza
fork	la forchetta
glass	il bicchiere
hungry (to be)	aver fame
knife	il coltello
matches	i fiammiferi

menu	il menu
mustard	la senape
napkin	la salvietta
oil	l'olio *m*
pepper	il pepe
plate	il piatto
salt	il sale
salt-cellar	la saliera
sauce	la salsa
saucer	il piattino
service	il servizio
spoon	il cucchiaio
table	la tavola
tablecloth	la tovaglia
thirsty (to be)	aver sete
tip	la mancia
toothpick	lo stuzzicadenti
vegetarian	vegetariano
vinegar	l'aceto *m*
waiter	il cameriere
waitress	la cameriera
water	l'acqua *f*
wine list	la lista dei vini

The Menu

MINESTRE	SOUPS
brodo di manzo	consommé
brodo di pollo	chicken broth
crema di piselli	cream of pea soup
crema di pollo	cream of chicken soup
fettuccine in brodo	noodle soup
minestra di cipolle	onion soup
minestra di fagioli	bean soup
minestra di lenticchie	lentil soup
minestra di pomodoro	tomato soup
minestra di riso	rice soup
minestrone	vegetable soup with noodles
pasta e fagioli	pasta and beans in broth
pasta in brodo	pasta in broth
stracciatella	broth with beaten egg, and cheese
taglierini in brodo	thin noodles in broth
zuppa di cozze	mussel soup
zuppa pavese	consommé with fried bread, poached egg and grated cheese
zuppa di verdura	vegetable soup

ANTIPASTI	HORS D'ŒUVRES
acciughe/alici	anchovies
antipasto misto	mixed hors d'œuvres
calamaretti	small squids
carciofini sott'olio	artichokes in olive oil
coppa	raw smoked ham
cozze	mussels
crostini di mare	shellfish on fried bread
datteri di mare	date-shells
finocchiona	fennel-flavoured salami
frutte di mare	shellfish salad
funghi sott'olio	mushrooms in olive oil
granchio	crab
insalata di finocchi e cetrioli	fennel and cucumber salad
insalata di funghi	salad of raw mushrooms
insalata di riso e scampi	salad of rice and scampi
insalata di tonno	tunny fish salad
lumache	snails
mortadella	mortadella, bologna sausage
olive	olives
ostriche	oysters
peperoni sott'olio	peppers in oil
pizza alla napoletana	pizza with tomato, anchovies, olives, capers and mozzarella

pizza alla siciliana	pizza with salami or ham, anchovies, tomato, olives and mozzarella
pomodori con tonno	tomatoes stuffed with tunny fish
prosciutto e melone	ham and melon
prosciutto e fichi	ham and figs
salame	salami
scampi	prawns
sardine	sardines
seppie	cuttlefish
tonno	tunny fish
totani	cuttlefish
uova sode agli spinaci	eggs Florentine
uova tonnate	hard boiled eggs in tunny sauce

PASTA ASCIUTTA	PASTA
cannelloni al forno	large macaroni, stuffed and browned in the oven
cappelletti	ringlets of pasta filled with minced meat
fettuccine	ribbon noodles
gnocchi alla piemontese	little balls of semolina and egg
gnocchi di patate	little balls of potato, flour and egg

lasagne (verdi) al forno	large strips of pasta (with spinach) browned in a sauce in the oven
maccheroni	macaroni
pappardelle al sugo di lepre	strips of pasta with hare sauce
penne/rigattoni	large macaroni
ravioli/tortelli	squares of pasta with a stuffing (usually meat)
spaghetti alla bolognese	spaghetti with meat sauce
spaghetti al pomodoro	spaghetti with tomato sauce
spaghetti alla vongole	spaghetti with clam sauce
tagliatelle alla bolognese	ribbon noodles with meat sauce
tortellini al sugo di carne	small ravioli with meat sauce

RISO	RICE
risi e bisi	rice with green peas
riso ai gamberi	boiled rice with shrimps
riso e ceci	a broth of rice and chick-peas with tomatoes and spices
riso alla genovese	rice with a sauce of minced beef or veal with vegetables
risotto alla marinara	rice with shrimps, squid and octopus
risotto alla milanese	rice with butter, saffron, beef marrow and Parmesan

risotto alla veronese	rice and ham with mushroom sauce
risotto di frutti di mare	shellfish risotto
risotto di peoci	risotto with mussels
risotto alla romana	risotto with mutton and tomatoes
supplì di riso	rice croquettes filled with ham and cheese

PESCE	FISH
anguille	eel
aragosta	rock lobster
baccalà	salt cod
calamari	squid
cefalo/muggine	grey mullet
fritto misto	mixed fried fish (squid, octopus and cuttle-fish)
gamberi	shrimps
granchio di mare	crab
merluzzo	hake
nasello	whiting
pesce alla griglia	grilled fish
pesce arrosto	roast fish
pesce fritto	fried fish
pesce San Pietro	John Dory

pesce spada	swordfish
polipi	octopus
ricci	sea urchins
rospo	monkfish
salmone	salmon
sardine	sardines
scampi	prawns
sgombro	mackerel
sogliola	sole
spigola	sea bass
storione	sturgeon
tonno	tunny
totani	cuttlefish
triglia	red mullet
trota	trout
ventresca	tunny fish belly

CARNE

MEAT

abbacchio/agnello	lamb
animella alla salvia	sweetbreads with sage
arista	roast loin of pork
bistecca alla pizzaiola	steak with tomato and garlic sauce
bollito	variety of boiled meats

capretto	kid
cervella	brain
cotoletta alla bolognese	fried veal cutlet with ham and tomato
cotoletta alla milanese	veal cutlet coated in egg and breadcrumbs and fried
fegato (alla veneziana)	liver (with onions)
filetto	fillet
girello	rump
lingua	tongue
maiale	pork
manzo	beef
manzo stufato al vino rosso	beef stewed in red wine
ossobuco alla milanese	stewed shin of veal with tomatoes, garlic and white wine
piccat di vitello	veal cooked with lemon and parsley
polpette	meat balls
polpettone	meat roll
porchetta	roast sucking pig
prosciutto affumicato	gammon
rognoncini al vino bianco	kidneys in white wine sauce
salsicce di maiale	pork sausages
saltimbocca alla romana	rolls of veal with ham

scaloppa milanese	escalope coated in egg and breadcrumbs, and fried
scaloppa napoletana	escalope coated in breadcrumbs and fried, with tomato sauce
scaloppine al marsala	small escalopes in marsala sauce
scaloppine al vino bianco	small escalopes in white wine sauce
spezzatino di vitello	veal stew
stracotto	beef stew with pork sausage
trippa	tripe
vitello	veal
vitello tonnato	cold veal with tunny fish sauce
zampone di maiole	stuffed pig's trotter

POLLAME E CACCIAGONE / POULTRY AND GAME

anitra	duck
cervo	venison
cinghiale	boar
coniglio	rabbit
fagiano	pheasant
faraona	guinea-fowl
lepre	hare
oca	goose
pernice	partridge
piccione	pigeon

pollo	chicken
quaglie	quails
tacchino	turkey
tordi	thrush
uccelletti	small birds of all kinds

CONTORNI

VEGETABLES AND SALAD

aglio	garlic
asparagi	asparagus
barbabietole	beetroot
carciofi	artichokes
carote	carrots
castagne	chestnuts
cavolfiore	cauliflower
cavoli	cabbage
cavolini di Bruxelles	Brussel sprouts
ceci	chick-peas
cetriolo	cucumber
cipolla	onion
fagioli	dried white beans
fagioli in erba	green beans
fave	broad beans
finocchio	fennel

funghi	mushrooms
insalata verde	green salad
lattuga	lettuce
lenticchie	lentils
melanzane	aubergine, egg plant
patate	potatoes
peperonata	tomatoes, peppers and onions stewed together
peperoni	peppers
piselli	peas
pomodoro	tomato
porro	leek
ravanelli	radishes
rape	turnip
scarola	chicory
sedano	celery
spinaci	spinach
zucchini	baby marrows

UOVA

EGGS

frittata	omelette
frittata al pomodoro	tomato omelette
frittata al prosciutto	ham omelette
frittata con spinaci	spinach omelette

uova al tegame con formaggio	fried eggs with cheese
uova moleette	soft boiled eggs
uova sode	hard boiled eggs
uova strapazzate	scrambled eggs

DOLCI

DESSERT

amaretti	macaroons
budino alla toscana	cream cheese with raisins, almonds, sugar and egg yolks
cassata alla siciliana	ice cream with candied fruit
gelato di cioccolato	chocolate ice cream
gelato di fragola	strawberry ice cream
gelato di limone	lemon ice cream
macedonia di frutta	fruit salad
Mont Blanc	puree of chestnuts with whipped cream
panettone	spiced bun with sultanas
panna montata	whipped cream
ricotta al maraschino	curd cheese with maraschino
tartufi di cioccolata	chocolate truffles
torrone	nougat
torta	gateau, cake
torta di cioccolata	chocolate cake
tortiglione	almond cakes

torta di mele	apple pie
zabaione	zabaglione
zuppa inglese	trifle

FRUTTA	**FRUIT**
albicocche	apricots
aranci	oranges
banana	banana
ciliege	cherries
cocomero/anguria	watermelon
datteri	dates
fichi	figs
fragole	strawberries
fragole di bosco	wild strawberries
lamponi	raspberries
manderini	tangerines
mandorle	almonds
mela	apple
melone	melon
noci	nuts
pera	pear
pesca	peach
pompelmo	grapefruit

prugna	plum
uva	grape

BEVANDE

DRINKS

acqua minerale	mineral water
amaro	bitters
aranciata	orangeade
birra	beer
brandy	brandy
caffé nero	black coffee
caffé e latte	white coffee
caffé con panna	coffee with cream
grappa	spirit made from grape pressings
limonata	lemonade
succo di frutta	fruit juice
vino	wine
bianco	white
rosso	red
dolce	sweet
secco	dry
spumante	sparkling

MODI DI COTTURA

WAYS OF COOKING

a vapore	steamed
affumicato	smoked
al burro	with butter

al forno	baked
al pesto	with basil, oil and garlic sauce
al ragù	stewed with vegetables
al sugo	with sauce
alla bolognese	with meat sauce
alla griglia	grilled
alla napoletana	with tomato sauce
alla panna	with cream
alla pizzaiola	with tomato and garlic sauce
arrosto	roast
bollito	boiled
carne – al sangue	meat – rare
media	medium
ben cotta	well done
con aglio	with garlic
con pomodoro	with tomato
crudo	raw
fritto	fried
in camicia	poached
in padella	fried
in umido	stewed
marinato	marinated
passato	pureed
ripieno	stuffed

salsa verde	sauce made from oil, lemon juice, capers, parsley and garlic
stufato	braised
trifolato	with truffles

Shopping[1] and services

Where to go

Where are the best department stores?	Dove sono i migliori magazzini?
Where is the market?	Dov'è il mercato?
Is there a market every day?	C'è mercato ogni giorno?
Where's the nearest chemist?	Dov'è la farmacia più vicina?
Can you recommend a ...?	Mi può raccomandare un ...?
Where can I buy ...?	Dove posso comprare ...?
When do the shops open/close?	A che ora aprono/chiudono i negozi?

baker	il panettiere	pa-net-tyair-ay
barber	il barbiere	bar-bee-air-ay
bookshop	la libreria	lee-brair-ee-a

1. Shops generally close at mid-day in Italy, and re-open at some point in the afternoon. The length of the mid-day break varies considerably from region to region, but is usually longer in the South than in the North.

butcher	la macelleria	ma-chel-lair-ee-a
cake shop	la pasticceria	pa-stee-chair-ee-a
chemist	la farmacia	far-ma-chee-a
dairy	la latteria	lat-tair-ee-a
department stores	i grandi magazzini	gran-dee ma-gad-zee-nee
delicatessen	la salumeria	sa-loo-mair-ee-a
dry cleaner	la pulitura a secco	poo-lee-too-ra a sek-ko
fishmonger	il pescivendolo	pe-shee-**ven**-doh-lo
florist	il fiorista	fee-or-ee-sta
greengrocer	il fruttivendolo	froot-tee-**ven**-doh-lo
grocer	la drogherià	drog-air-ee-a
haberdashery	la merceria	mer-chair-ee-a
hairdresser	il parrucchiere	par-rook-kyair-ay
hardware shop	il negozio di ferramenta	ne-go-tsee-o dee fer-ra-men-ta
jeweller	la gioielleria	joy-el-lai-ree-a
launderette/laundry	la lavanderia	la-van-dai-ree-a
newsagent	il giornalaio	jor-nal-a-yo
optician	l'ottico *m*	**ot**-tee-ko
shoe repairer	il calzolaio	kal-tsol-a-yo
shoe shop	il negozio di calzature	ne-**go**-tsee-o dee kalt-za-too-ray
stationer	la cartoleria	kar-to-lair-ee-a
tobacconist	la tabaccheria	ta-bak-kair-ee-a

| toy shop | il negozio di giocattoli | ne-go-tsee-o dee jo-kat-to-lee |

In the shop

Self service	*Self-service
Sale (clearance)	*La svendita
Cash desk	*Cassa
Shop assistant	Commesso/commessa
Manager	Direttore
Can I help you?	*In cosa posso servirla?
I want to buy ...	Vorrei comprare ...
Do you sell ...?	Vende ...?
I just want to look round	Vorrei solo dare un'occhiata in giro
I don't want to buy anything now	Non compro niente adesso
Could you show me ...?	Può farmi vedere ...?
You'll find them at that counter	*Li troverà a quel banco
We've sold out but we'll have more tomorrow	*Sono finiti ma li riceveremo domani
Anything else?	*Nient'altro?
That will be all	Questo è tutto
Will you take it with you?	*Lo prende adesso?

Please send them to this address/ X hotel

Per favore li mandi a questo indirizzo/all'albergo X

Choosing

I want something in leather/green

Vorrei qualcosa in pelle/di color verde

I need it to match this

Voglio che vada bene con questo

What colour do you want?

*Che colore desidera?

I don't like this colour

Non mi piace questo colore

I like the colour but want a different style

Il colore va bene ma vorrei uno stile diverso

I like the one in the window

Mi piace quello in vetrina

I want a darker/lighter shade

Vorrei una tinta più scura/più chiara

I need something warmer/thinner

Vorrei qualcosa di più pesante/ più leggero

Do you have one in another colour/size?

Ha niente in un colore diverso/ di un'altra taglia?

Have you anything better/ cheaper?

Vorrei qualcosa di meglio/ meno costoso

Could I see that one, please?

Posso vedere quello, per favore?

How much is this?

Quanto costa?

I am sorry, that's too much for me

Mi dispiace, costa troppo

What's it made of?	Di cosa è fatto?
For how long is it guaranteed?	Per quanto tempo è garantito?
Can I try it on?	Posso provarlo?
It's too short/long/tight/loose	È troppo corto/lungo/stretto/largo
Have you a larger/smaller one?	Ne ha uno più grande/più piccolo?
What size?[1]	*Di che misura?
I want size ...	Voglio la misura ...
The English/American size is ...	La misura inglese/americana è ...
My collar size is ...	Il mio numero di colletto è ...
My chest measurement is ...	Il mio numero di petto è ...
My waist measurement is ...	Il mio numero di cintura è ...

Colours

beige	beige	
black	nero	ne-ro
blue	blu	bloo
brown	marrone	mar-ro-nay
gold	oro	or-o

1. See p. 106 for Continental sizes.

green	verde	ver-day
grey	grigio	gree-jo
orange	arancione	a-ran-chio-nay
pink	rosa	ro-sa
purple	porpora	por-por-a
red	rosso	ros-so
silver	argento	ar-jen-toh
white	bianco	byan-ko
yellow	giallo	jal-lo

Complaints

I want to see the manager	Desidero vedere il direttore
I bought this yesterday	L'ho comprato ieri
It doesn't work	Non funziona
It does not fit	Non è la misura giusta
This is dirty/stained/torn/broken/cracked	E sporco/macchiato/strappato/rotto/spaccato
Will you change it, please?	Lo può cambiare, per favore?
Will you refund my money?	Mi può restituire il denaro?
Here is the receipt	Ecco la ricevuta

Paying

That's 6,000 lire, please	*Costa sei mila lire
They are 100 lire each	*Costano cento lire l'uno
It's too expensive	E troppo caro
Don't you have anything cheaper?	Non ha niente di meno costoso?
Will you take English/American currency?	Posso pagare in sterline/in dollari?
Do you take travellers' cheques?	Accetta travellers' cheques?
Please pay the cashier	*Si accomodi alla cassa, per favore
May I have a receipt, please?	Mi può rilasciare una ricevuta, per favore?
You've given me too little/too much change	Mi ha dato meno di resto/mi ha dato troppo
How much does that come to?	Quanto è tra tutto?
That will be . . .	*Fa . . ./Sono . . .

Chemist[1]

Can you prepare this prescription for me, please?	Mi può preparare questa ricetta, per favore?

1. See also AT THE DOCTOR'S (p. 131).

Have you a small first-aid kit?	Ha una valigetta di pronto soccorso?
A bottle of aspirin, please	Una boccetta di aspirine, per favore
A tin of adhesive plaster	Una scatolina di cerotti
Can you suggest something for indigestion/constipation/diarrhoea?	Mi può indicare qualcosa contro l'indigestione/la stitichezza/la diarrea?
I want something for insect bites	Voglio qualcosa contro i morsi degli insetti
Can you give me something for sunburn?	Mi può dare qualcosa contro le bruciature di sole?
I want some throat/cough lozenges	Vorrei delle pasticche per la gola/per la tosse
I need something for a hangover/sea sickness	Vorrei qualcosa contro il mal di testa/il mal di mare
I want some antiseptic cream/lip salve	Vorrei della crema antisettica/della pomata per le labbra

Toilet requisites

A packet of razor blades, please	Un pacchetto di lamette da barba, per favore
Have you an after-shave lotion?	Ha una lozione per barba?
How much is this lotion?	Quanto costa questa lozione?

A tube of toothpaste, please

Un dentifricio, per favore

Give me a box of paper handkerchiefs, please

Mi dia una scatola di fazzoletti di carta, per favore

I want some eau-de-cologne/ perfume

Vorrei dell'acqua di Colonia/ un profumo

What kinds of soap have you?

Che tipi di saponi avete?

A bottle/tube of shampoo, please, for normal/dry/greasy hair

Una bottiglia/una bustina di shampoo per capelli normali/ secchi/grassi

Do you sell sanitary towels/ tampons/cotton wool?

Vende assorbenti igienici/ tamponi/cotone?

Do you have any suntan oil/ cream?

Ha qualche lozione/crema abbronzante?

Sun cream for children

Crema solare per ragazzi

Toilet paper

Carta igienica

Clothes and shoes[1]

I want a hat/sunhat

Vorrei un cappello/un cappello da sole

I'd like a pair of white cotton gloves/black leather gloves

Vorrei un paio di guanti di filo bianco/di pelle nera

Can I see some dresses, please?

Potrei vedere qualche abito, per favore?

1. For sizes see p. 106.

Where's the coat department?	Dove sono i soprabiti?
Where are beach clothes?	Dove sono gli abiti da spiaggia?
The men's department is on the second floor	Le confezioni per uomo sono al secondo piano
Where is the underwear/haberdashery department?	Dov'è il reparto della biancheria intima/il reparto merceria?
Where can I find stockings/socks?	Dov'è che vendono calze/calzini?
I am looking for a blouse/bra/dress/jumper	Cerco una blusa/un reggipetto/un vestito/una maglietta
I need a coat/raincoat/jacket/pair of trousers	Ho bisogno di un soprabito/un impermeabile/una giacchetta/un paio di calzoni
I want a short/long sleeved shirt, collar size . . .	Voglio una camicia a maniche corte/lunghe, colletto numero . . .
Do you sell buttons/elastic/zips?	Vende bottoni/elastico/cerniere?
I need a pair of walking shoes	Ho bisogno di un paio di scarpe da passeggio
I need a pair of beach sandals/black shoes	Ho bisogno di un paio di sandali da spiaggia/scarpe nere
These heels are too high/too low	Questi tacchi sono troppo alti/troppo bassi

Clothing sizes

WOMEN'S DRESSES, ETC.

British	32	34	36	38	40	42	44
American	10	12	14	16	18	20	22
Continental	38	40	42	44	46	48	50

MEN'S SUITS

British and American	36	38	40	42	44	46
Continental	46	48	50	52	54	56

MEN'S SHIRTS

British and American	14	14½	15	15½	16	16½	17
Continental	36	37	38	39	41	42	43

STOCKINGS

British and American	8	8½	9	9½	10	10½	11
Continental	0	1	2	3	4	5	6

SOCKS

British and American	9½	10	10½	11	11½
Continental	38–39	39–40	40–41	41–42	42–43

SHOES

British	1	2	3	4	5	6	7	8	9	10	11	12
American	2½	3½	4½	5½	6½	7½	8½	9½	10½	11½	12½	13½
Continental	33	34–5	36	37	38	39–40	41	42	43	44	45	46

Food[1]

Give me a kilo/half a kilo of . . ., please	Vuol darmi un chilo/mezzo chilo di . . ., per favore
I want some sweets/chocolate, please	Vorrei dei dolciumi/una cioccolata, per favore
A bottle of milk	Una bottiglia di latte
Is there anything back on the bottle?	C'è un rimborso sulla bottiglia?
A litre/half a litre of wine	Un litro/mezzo litro di vino
A bottle of beer	Una bottiglia di birra
I want a jar/tin/packet of . . .	Vorrei un barattolo/una scatolina un pacchetto di . . .
Do you sell frozen foods?	Vende cibi congelati?
These pears are too hard/soft	Queste pere non sono ancora mature/sono troppo mature

1. See also the various MENU sections (p. 81 onwards) and WEIGHTS AND MEASURES (p. 155).

Is it fresh?	E fresco?
Are they ripe?	Sono mature?
This is bad/stale	Questa è marcia/andata a male
A loaf of bread, please	Un filone di pane, per favore
How much a kilo/a litre?	Quanto costa al chilo/al litro?

Hairdresser and barber

May I make an appointment for tomorrow/this afternoon?	Posso fissare un appuntamento per domani/per questo pomeriggio?
What time?	A che ora?
I want my hair cut/trimmed	Mi vuol tagliare/spuntare i capelli, per favore
Not too short at the sides	Non troppo corti ai lati
I'll have it shorter at the back, please	Può farmeli un po' più corti sul collo?
My hair is oily/dry/normal	Ho i capelli grassi/secchi/normali
I want a shampoo	Vorrei uno shampoo
I want my hair washed and set	Mi vuol lavare i capelli e fare la messa in piega, per favore
Please set it without rollers	Per favore, mi faccia la messa in piega senza bigodini

Please set it on large/small rollers	Per favore, mi faccia la messa in piega con bigodini grossi/ piccoli
I want a dark rinse	Vorrei un colore scuro
I'd like to see a colour chart	Vorrei vedere la gamma delle tinte
I want my hair tinted	Vorrei farmi tingere i capelli
I want a darker/lighter shade	Vorrei una tinta più scura/più chiara
I want my hair permed/waved	Vorrei la permanente/capelli ondulati
I'd like it set this way, please	Vorrei una messa in piega così, per favore
Have you any lacquer?	Ha una lacca?
The water is too cold	L'acqua è troppo fredda
The dryer is too hot	Il casco è troppo caldo
Thank you, I like it very much	Grazie, mi piace moltissimo
I want a shave/manicure	Vuol farmi la barba, per favore/ Vorrei la manicure
Shave and hair cut	Barba e capelli

Hardware

Where is the camping equipment?	Dove sono le attrezzature da campeggio?
Do you have a battery for this?	Ha una batteria per questo?
Where can I get butane gas/paraffin?	Dove posso trovare del gas butano/della paraffina?
I need a bottle opener/tin opener/corkscrew	Mi occorre un apribottiglie/un apriscatole/un cavatappi
I'd like some candles and a box of matches	Vorrei delle candele e una scatola di fiammiferi
I want a flashlight/knife/pair of scissors	Vorrei una torcia elettrica/un coltello/un paio di forbici
A small/large screwdriver	Un cacciavite grande/piccolo
Do you sell string/rope?	Vende dello spago/della corda?
Where can I find washing-up liquid/soap?	Dove posso trovare un detersivo per i piatti/del sapone?
Do you have a dishcloth/broom?	Ha uno strofinaccio/una scopa?
I want a bucket/frying pan	Mi occorre un secchiello/una padella

Laundry and dry cleaning

Where is the nearest launderette/dry cleaner?	Dov'è la più vicina lavanderia automatica/lavanderia a secco?
I want to have these things washed/cleaned	Vorrei far lavare/pulire a secco queste cose
Can you get this stain out?	Può togliere questa macchia?
It is coffee/wine/grease	E caffè/vino/grasso
These stains won't come out	*Queste macchie non vanno via
It only needs to be pressed	Ha solo bisogno di essere stirato
This is torn; can you mend it?	Questo è rotto. Può rammendarlo?
Do you do invisible mending?	Può fare un rammendo invisibile?
There's a button missing	Ci manca un bottone
Can you sew on a button here, please?	Può attacare un bottone qui, per favore?
When will they be ready?	Quando saranno pronti/pronte?
I need them by this evening/tomorrow	Ne avrei bisogno per questa sera/domani
Call back at 5 o'clock	*Torni alle cinque
We can do it by Tuesday	*Possiamo farlo per martedì
It will take three days	*Ci vorranno tre giorni

Newspapers, writing materials, records

Do you sell English/American newspapers	Vende giornali inglesi/ americani?
Can you get this magazine for me?	Può ordinare questa rivista per me?
I want a map of the city	Vorrei una mappa della città
Do you have any English books?	Vende libri inglesi?
Have you any novels by . . .?	Ha qualche romanzo di . . .?
I want some picture postcards/ plain postcards	Vorrei delle cartoline illustrate/ cartoline postali
Do you sell souvenirs/toys?	Vende dei ricordi/giocattoli?
Do you have any records of local music?	Ha dischi di musica locale?
Can I listen to this record, please?	Posso sentire questo disco, per favore?

Photography

I want to buy a camera	Vorrei comprare una macchina fotografica
Have you a film/cartridge for this camera?	Ha una pellicola/un rotolo per questa macchina?

A 120 . . . film, please	Una pellicola di cento venti . . ., per favore
Give me a 35 mm. colour film with 20/36 exposures	Mi dia una pellicola a colori di trentacinque millimetri con venti/trentasei esposizioni
I want a colour film/black and white film	Voglio una pellicola per fotografie a colori/in bianco e nero
Would you fit the film in the camera for me, please?	Può aggiustarmi la pellicola nella macchina, per favore?
Do you sell flash cubes?	Ha lampi al magnesio?
How much is it?	Quanto è?
Does the price include processing?	Lo sviluppo è compreso nel prezzo?
I'd like this film developed and printed	Vorrei far sviluppare e stampare queste fotografie
Please enlarge this negative	Vorrei far ingrandire questa fotografia
When will they be ready?	Quando saranno pronte?
Will they be done tomorrow?	Saranno pronte per domani?
My camera's not working, can you mend it?	La mia macchina non funziona. Può accomodarla?
There is something wrong with the shutter/light meter	L'otturatore/il fotometro non funziona bene
The film is jammed	La pellicola non scorre

Tobacconist

Do you stock English/American cigarettes?	Vende sigarette inglesi/americane?
What English cigarettes have you?	Che sigarette inglesi ha?
A packet of . . ., please	Un pacchetto di . . ., per favore
I want some filter tip cigarettes/cigarettes without filter/mentholated cigarettes	Vorrei delle sigarette con filtro/senza filtro/mentolate
A box of matches, please	Una scatola di fiammiferi, per favore
Do you have cigarette papers/pipe cleaners?	Ha cartine per sigarette/qualcosa per pulir la pipa?
I want to buy a lighter	Vorrei comprare un accendisigaro
Do you sell lighter fuel/flints?	Vende benzina/pietrine per accendisigaro?
I want a gas refill for this lighter	Vorrei un bomboletta di gas per questo accendisigaro

Repairs

This is broken, could somebody mend it?	Questo è rotto. Può ripararlo?
I want these shoes soled (in leather)	Vorrei far risuolare queste scarpe (in cuoio)

Can you heel these shoes (with rubber)?	Può mettere dei tacchi (di gomma) a queste scarpe?
I have broken the heel; can you put on a new one?	Il tacco è rotto; può metterne uno nuovo?
My watch is broken	Mi si è rotto l'orologio
My watch is always fast/slow	Il mio orologio va sempre avanti/indietro
Can you repair it?	Può ripararlo?
I've broken the strap	Mi si è rotto il cinturino
The fastener/clip/chain is broken	La chiusura/la molletta/la catena è rotta
The charm has come loose	Il ciondolo si è allentato
The stone is loose	La gemma non è ben fissa
I have broken my glasses/the frame	Mi si sono rotti gli occhiali/mi si è rotta la montatura
How much will it cost?	Quanto mi verrà a costare?
How much will a new one cost?	Quanto costerebbe nuovo?
It can't be repaired	*Non si può riprarare
You need a new one	*Deve comprarne uno nuovo
Can you do them while I wait?	Può farlo mentre aspetto?
When should I pick them up?	Quando debbo venire a ritirarli?

Post Office

Where's the main post office?	Dov'è l'ufficio postale centrale?
Where's the nearest post office?	Dov'è l'ufficio postale più vicino?
What time does the post office open/close?	A che ora apre/chiude l'ufficio postale?
Where's the post box?	Dov'è una buca per le lettere?
Which window do I go to for telegrams/stamps/money orders?	Quale è lo sportello per i telegrammi/per i francobolli/ per mandare vaglia postali?

Letters and telegrams

How much is a letter to England?	Che francobollo ci vuole per l'Inghilterra?

What's the airmail to the USA?	Quanto costa una lettera per via aerea per gli Stati Uniti?
It's inland	Per l'interno
Give me three . . . lire stamps, please	Vorrei tre francobolli da . . . lire
I want to send this letter express	Voglio mandare questa lettera espresso
I want to register this letter	Voglio mandare questa lettera raccomandata
Two airmail forms, please	Due moduli per posta aerea, per favore
Where is the poste restante section?	Dov'è lo sportello del Fermo Posta?
Are there any letters for me?	Vi sono lettere per me?
What is your name?	*Il suo nome, per favore
Have you any means of identification?	*Ha qualche documento di identità?
I want to send a telegram/ reply paid/overnight	Debbo mandare un telegramma/ un telegramma con risposta pagata/un telegramma E.L.T.
How much does it cost per word?	Quanto costa a parola?
Write the message here and your own name and address	*Scriva qui il testo col suo nome e indirizzo

Telephoning

Where's the nearest phone box?	Dov'è la più vicina cabina telefonica?
I want to make a phone call	Voglio fare una telefonata
May I use your phone?	Posso usare questo telefono?
Do you have a telephone directory for . . .?	Ha l'elenco telefonico di . . .?
Please give me . . . tokens	Può darmi . . . gettoni, per favore
Please get me Milan . . .	Desidero chiamare Milano . . .
I want to telephone to England	Voglio telefonare in Inghilterra
I want to make a personal call	Voglio fare una chiamata personale
Could you give me the costs?	Può dirmi quanto costa?
I want to reverse the charges/ call collect	Vorrei fare una rovesciata
We were cut off, can you reconnect me?	Ci hanno interrotto. Può rimettermi in linea?
Hallo	Pronto
I want extension . . .	Voglio parlare coll' interno . . .
May I speak to . . .	Posso parlare con . . .
Who's speaking?	Chi parla?
Hold the line, please	*Rimanga in linea, prego
Put the receiver down	*Abbassi il ricevitore
He's not here	*Non è qui

He's at . . .	*E a . . .
When will he be back?	Quando sarà di ritorno?
Will you take a message?	Posso lasciare un messaggio?
Tell him that . . . phoned	Gli dica che gli ha telefonato . . .
Please ask him to phone me	Per favore, gli dica di telefonarmi
What's your number?	*Quale è il suo numero?
My number is . . .	Il mio numero è . . .
I can't hear you	Non sento
The line is engaged	*La linea è occupata
There's no reply	*Non c'è risposta
You have the wrong number	*Il suo numero è sbagliato

Sightseeing[1]

What ought one to see here?	Cosa c'è di interessante da vedere qui?
Is there a sightseeing tour?	C'è un giro organizzato della città?
Are there boat rides?	Ci sono giri in barca organizzati?
What's this building?	Cos'è questo edificio?
Which is the oldest building in the city?	Quale è il più antico edificio della città?
When was it built?	Quando fu costruito?
Who built it?	Chi lo costruì?
What's the name of this church?	Che chiesa è questa?
What time is mass at . . . church?	A che ora dicono la Messa alla chiesa di . . .?
What time is the service?	A che ora comincia la funzione?
Where is the English church/synagogue?	Dov'è la chiesa anglicana/la sinagoga?

1. See also TRAVEL (Bus or Coach) (p. 45) and DIRECTIONS (p. 48).

Please cover your head	*Si metta qualcosa in testa, per favore
Is this the natural history museum?	E il museo di storia naturale?
When is the museum open?	A che ora apre il museo?
Is it open on Sundays?	E aperto la domenica?
The museum is closed on Mondays	*Il museo è chiuso il lunedì
Admission free	*Ingresso libero
How much is it to go in?	Quanto costa il biglietto d'entrata?
Are there reductions for students/ children under 12?	Ci sono riduzioni per studenti/ per ragazzi sotto i dodici anni?
Which days is admission free?	In quali giorni c'è ingresso libero?
Have you a ticket?	*Ha il biglietto?
Where do I get tickets?	Dove si comprano i biglietti?
Please leave your bag in the cloakroom	*Lasci la cartella nel guardaroba, per favore
It's over there	*E da questa parte
Can I take pictures?	Si possono prendere fotografie?
Photographs are prohibited	*E vietato prendere fotografie
Follow the guide	*Segua la guida
Does the guide speak English?	Parla inglese la guida?
I don't need a guide	Grazie, non ho bisogno di guida

Where is the X collection/
exhibition?

Dov'è la collezione/esposizione
X?

Where are the Titians?

In che sala sono i quadri di
Tiziano?

Where can I get a catalogue?

Dove posso comprare un
catalogo?

Where can I get a map/guide
book of the city?

Dove posso comprare una
mappa/una guida della città?

Is this the way to the zoo?

E questa la strada per il
giardino zoologico?

Which bus goes to the castle?

Quale è l'autobus per il
castello?

Which is the way to the park?

Quale è la strada per il parco?

Where do we find antiques/
souvenirs?

Dove possiamo trovare oggetti
d'antiquariato/dei ricordi?

Where is the shopping centre/
market?

Dove sono i negozi/dov'è il
mercato?

Can we walk there?

Possiamo andarci a piedi?

Entertainment

Is there an entertainment guide?	C'è una guida degli spettacoli?
What's on at the theatre/cinema?	Cosa danno al teatro/al cinema?
Is there a concert on this evening?	C'è un concerto stasera?
I want two seats for tonight/ the matinée tomorrow	Due posti per stasera/per la matinée di domani
I want to book seats for Thursday	Vorrei riservare dei posti per giovedì
We've sold out (for that performance)	*Tutto esaurito (per questa rappresentazione)
Where are these seats?	Dove si trovano questi posti?
What time does the performance start?	A che ora comincia lo spettacolo?
What time does it end?	A che ora finisce?
Is evening dress necessary?	È necessario l'abito da sera?
Where is the cloakroom?	Dov'è il guardaroba?
This is your seat	*Ecco il Suo posto

A programme, please	Un programma, per favore
Where are the best nightclubs?	Dove sono i migliori locali notturni?
What time is the floorshow/ the cabaret?	A che ora comincia lo spettacolo/il cabaret?
Can I have this dance?	Posso invitarLa a ballare?
Is there a discotheque here?	C'è una discoteca qui?
Can you recommend a good show?	Può raccomandarmi un buon spettacolo?

Sports and games

Where is the nearest tennis court/ golf course?

Dov'è il più vicino campo da tennis/campo di golf?

What is the charge per game/ hour/day?

Quanto si paga per partita/ all'ora/a giornata?

Where can we go swimming/ fishing?

Dove si può andare per far bagni/per pescare?

Can I hire a racket/clubs/ fishing tackle?

È possibile noleggiare una racchetta/mazze da golf/ arnesi da pesca?

Do I need a permit?

Occorre un permesso speciale?

Where do I get a permit?

Chi rilascia questo permesso?

Is there a skating rink?

C'è una pista per pattinaggio?

Can I hire skates/ski-ing equipment?

Posso noleggiare i pattini/ l'attrezzatura da sci?

Are there ski lifts?

Vi sono sciovie?

Can I take lessons here?

Danno anche lezioni?

Where is the stadium?

Dov'è lo stadio?

Are there still any seats in the grandstand?	Ci sono ancora posti in tribuna?
How much are they?	Quanto costano?
Which are the cheapest seats?	Quali sono i posti meno costosi?
Are the seats in the sun/shade?	Questi posti/sono al sole/all'ombra?
We want to go to a football match/the tennis tournament	Vogliamo andare a una partita di calcio/al torneo di tennis
Who's playing?	Chi giuoca?
When does it start?	Quando comincia?
What is the score?	Quale è il punteggio?
Who's winning?	Chi vince?
Where's the race course?	Dove sono le corse di cavalli?
When's the next meeting?	Quando sarà il prossimo incontro?
Which is the favourite?	Chi è il favorito?
Who's the jockey?	Chi è il fantino?
1000 lire on . . .	Mille lire su . . .
What are the odds?	Quale è la posta?
Do you play cards?	Giuoca a carte?
Would you like a game of chess?	Ha voglia di fare una partita a scacchi?
I'll give you a game of checkers if you like	Posso fare una partita a dama, se vuole

On the beach

Where are the best beaches?	Dove sono le migliori spiagge?
Is there a quiet beach near here?	C'è una spiaggia tranquilla qui vicino?
Can we walk or is it too far?	Ci si può andare a piedi o è troppo lontana?
Is there a bus to the beach?	C'è un autobus per andare alla spiaggia?.
Is the beach sand or shingle?	La spiaggia è sabbia o ghiaia?
Is it dangerous to bathe here?	E pericoloso fare bagni qui?
Is it safe for children?	E sicura questa spiaggia per i ragazzi?
Is diving dangerous from these rocks? *	E pericoloso tuffarsi da questi scogli?
Bathing prohibited	*Vietato fare bagni
Diving prohibited	*Vietato tuffarsi
It's dangerous	*E pericoloso
There's a strong current here	*C'è una forte corrente qui

Are you a strong swimmer?	*Nuota bene Lei?
Is it deep?	E profonda l'acqua qui?
How's the water? Cold?	Come è l'acqua? Fredda?
It's warm	E tiepida
Can one swim in the lake/river?	Si può fare un bagno nel lago/nel fiume?
Is there an indoor/outdoor swimming pool?	C'è una piscina coperta/all'aperto?
Is it salt or fresh water?	E acqua salata o dolce?
Are there showers?	Ci sono docce?
I want a cabin for the day/for the morning/for two hours	Vorrei una cabina per oggi soltanto/per stamani/per due ore
I want to hire a deckchair/sunshade	Vorrei noleggiare una sedia a sdraio/un ombrellone
Can we water-ski here?	Si può fare sci nautico qui?
Can we hire the equipment?	Possiamo prendere a nolo l'attrezzatura?
Where's the harbour?	Dov'è il porto?
Can we go out in a fishing boat?	Si può andare in un battello da pesca?
We want to go fishing	Vorremmo andare a pescare
Is there any underwater fishing?	Si può fare pesca subacquea?
Can I hire a boat?	Si può noleggiare una barca?
What does it cost by the hour?	Quanto costa all'ora?

Camping and walking[1]

How long is the walk to the Youth Hostel?

Quanto ci vuole per andare a piedi all'Ostello della Gioventù?

How far is the next village?

Quanto c'è di qui al prossimo paese?

Is there a footpath to . . .?

C'è un sentiero per . . .?

Is there a short cut?

C'è una scorciatoia?

It's an hour's walk to . . .

*Ci vuole un'ora a piedi di qui a . . .

Is there a camping site near here?

C'è un campeggio qui vicino?

Is this an authorized camp site?

E questo un campeggio autorizzato?

Is there drinking water?

C'è acqua potabile?

Are there lavatories/showers?

Ci sono gabinetti/docce?

May we camp here?

Ci possiamo accampare qui?

Can we hire a tent?

Si può noleggiare una tenda?

1. See also DIRECTONS (p. 48).

Can we park our caravan here?

Si può parcheggiare la roulotte qui?

What does it cost per person/ day/week?

Quanto si paga a persona/per un giorno/per una settimana?

What is the charge for a tent/ caravan?

Quanto costa noleggiare una tenda/una roulotte?

Is this drinking water?

E potabile quest'acqua?

Where are the shops?

Dove sono i negozi?

Where can I buy paraffin/ butane gas?

Dove posso comprare della paraffina/del gas butano?

May we light a fire?

Si può accendere il fuoco?

Where do I dispose of rubbish?

Dove si buttano le immondizie?

At the doctor's

Ailments

Is there a doctor's surgery near here?	C'è un ambulatorio medico qui vicino?
I must see a doctor, can you recommend one?	Debbo vedere un dottore. Può raccomandarmene uno?
Please call a doctor	Mi vuol chiamare un dottore, per favore?
I am ill	Mi sento poco bene
I've a pain in my arm	Ho un dolore al braccio
My wrist hurts	Ho male al polso
I think I've sprained/broken my ankle	Credo di essermi slogata/rotta la caviglia
I fell down and hurt my back	Sono caduto e mi sono fatto male alla schiena
My feet are swollen	Ho i piedi gonfi

I've burned/cut/bruised myself	Mi sono bruciato/tagliato/ammaccato
My stomach is upset	Ho mal di stomaco
I have indigestion	Ho preso una indigestione
My appetite's gone	Non ho appetito
I think I've got food poisoning	Credo di aver mangiato del cibo avariato
I can't eat/sleep	Non posso mangiare/dormire
I am a diabetic	Ho il diabete
My nose keeps bleeding	Mi esce sangue dal naso
I have earache	Ho mal d'orecchi
I have difficulty in breathing	Provo difficoltà a respirare
I feel dizzy	Mi gira la testa
I feel sick/shivery	Ho la nausea/mi vengono i brividi
I feel sick	Sento nausea
I keep vomiting	Mi viene spesso da vomitare
I think I've caught 'flu	Credo di aver preso l'influenza
I've got a heavy cold	Ho un forte raffreddore
I've had it since yesterday	Sono due giorni che ho il raffreddore
I've had it for a few hours	L'ho da alcune ore
abscess l'ascesso *m*	a-shes-so

ache	il dolore	do-lo-ray
allergy	l'allergia *f*	al-lair-jee-a
appendicitis	l'appendicite *f*	ap-pen-dee-chee-tay
asthma	l'asma	as-ma
blister	la vescica	ve-shee-ka
boil	il foruncolo	for-roon-ko-lo
bruise	l'ammaccatura *f*	am-mak-kat-oo-ra
burn	la bruciatura	broo-cha-too-ra
chill	il colpo di freddo	kol-po dee fred-doh
cold	il raffreddore	raf-fred-dor-ay
constipation	la stitichezza	stee-tee-ket-za
cough	la tosse	tos-say
cramp	il crampo	kram-po
diabetic *adj.*	diabetico	dee-a-be-tee-ko
diarrhoea	la diarrea	dee-ar-ray-a
earache	il mal d'orecchi	mal do-rek-ee
fever	la febbre	feb-bray
fracture	la frattura	frat-too-ra
hay fever	la febbre del fieno	feb-bray del fee-ay-no
headache	il mal di testa	mal dee tes-ta
ill, sick	ammalato	am-ma-la-toh
illness	la malattia	ma-lat-tee-a
indigestion	l'indigestione *f*	een-dee-jest-yo-nay

infection	i'infezione *f*	een-fets-yo-nay
influenza	l'influenza *f*	een-floo-en-za
insomnia	l'insonnia *f*	een-son-nee-a
pain	il dolore	do-lo-ray
rheumatism	il reumatismo	roo-ma-tees-mo
sore throat	il mal di gola	mal dee go-la
stomach ache	il mal di stomaco	mal dee stó-ma-ko
sunburn	la scottatura di sole	skot-tat-oo-ra dee so-lay
sunstroke	il colpo di sole	kol-po dee so-lay
toothache	il mal di denti	mal dee den-tee
ulcer	l'ulcera	ool-se-ra
wound	la ferita	fe-ree-ta

Treatment

I feel better now	Adesso mi sento meglio
Did you take your temperature?	*Si è misurata la temperatura?
Does that hurt?	*Le fa male?
A lot or a little?	*Tanto o poco?
Where does it hurt?	*Dove Le fa male?
Have you a pain here?	*Le fa male qui?
How long have you had the pain/been suffering from . . .?	*Da quanto tempo ha questo dolore/soffre di . . .?

Open your mouth	*Vuole aprire la bocca, per favore
Put out your tongue	*Mi faccia vedere la lingua
Breathe in	*Respiri
Hold your breath	*Trattenga il respiro
I will need a blood specimen	*Mi occorre un campione del sangue
What medicines are you taking?	*Che medicine prende?
I take this medicine – could you give me another prescription?	Prendo questa medicina. Mi potrebbe fare un'altra ricetta?
I will give you an antibiotic/sedative	*Le ordinerò degli antibiotici/un calmante
Please lie down	*Si sdrai, La prego
Take these pills/medicine	*Prenda queste pillole/questa medicina
Take this prescription to the chemist's	*Porti questa ricetta alla farmacia
Take this three times a day	*Prenda questa medicina tre volte al giorno
I'll give you an injection	*Le faccio una iniezione
Roll up your sleeve	*Si tiri su la manica
You should stick to a diet for a few days	*Lei deve stare a dieta per alcuni giorni
Come and see me again in two days' time	*Torni da me tra due giorni
Your leg must be X-rayed	*Deve farsi fare i raggi X a questa gamba

You must go to hospital — *Deve ricoverarsi in ospedale

You must stay in bed for a few days — *Deve rimanere a letto per alcuni giorni

You're hurting me — Mi fa male

Must I stay in bed? — Debbo rimanere a letto?

Will you come and see me again? — Torna di nuovo a farmi una visita?

When do you think I can leave? — Quando crede che possa partire?

You should not travel for at least ... days — *Non si metta in viaggio per almeno ... giorni

Nothing to worry about — *Niente di preoccupante

How much do I owe you? — Quanto Le debbo?

ambulance	l'ambulanza f	am-boo-lant-sa
anaesthetic	l'anestetico m	an-es-te-tee-ko
aspirin	l'aspirina f	as-pee-ree-na
bandage	la fascia	fa-shia
chiropodist	il pedicure	pe-dee-koo-ráy
hospital	l'ospedale m	os-pe-da-lay
injection	l'iniezione f	een-yet-syo-nay
laxative	il lassativo	las-sa-tee-vo
nurse	l'infermiera f	een-fair-mee-air-a
operation	l'operazione f	op-air-at-zyo-nay
optician	l'ottico m	ot-tee-ko

pill	la pastiglia	pas-tee-lya
(adhesive) plaster	il cerotto	che-rot-toh
prescription	la ricetta	ree-chet-ta
X-ray	i raggi X	rad-jee eeks

Parts of the body

ankle	la caviglia	ka-vee-lya
arm	il braccio	bra-chyo
back	il dorso	dor-so
bladder	la vescica	ve-shee-ka
blood	il sangue	san-gway
body	il corpo	kor-po
brain	il cervello	chair-vel-lo
cheek	la guancia	gwan-cha
chest	il petto	pet-toh
chin	il mento	men-toh
ear	l'orecchio *m*	or-rek-kyo
elbow	il gomito	go-mee-toh
eye	l'occhio *m*	ok-kyo
face	la faccia	fa-chya
finger	il dito	dee-toh

foot	il piede	pee-ay-day
forehead	la fronte	fron-tay
gum	la gengiva	jen-jee-va
hand	la mano	ma-no
head	la testa	tes-ta
heart	il cuore	kwor-ay
heel	il tallone	tal-lo-nay
hip	il fianco	fee-an-ko
jaw	la mascella	ma-shel-la
kidney	il rene	ray-nay
knee	il ginocchio	jee-nok-kyo
leg	la gamba	gam-ba
lip	il labbro	lab-bro
liver	il fegato	fe-ga-toh
lung	il polmone	pol-mo-nay
mouth	la bocca	bok-ka
muscle	il muscolo	moos-ko-lo
nail	l'unghia	oong-ya
neck	il collo	kol-lo
nerve	il nervo	nair-vo
nose	il naso	na-so
rib	la costola	kos-to-la
shoulder	la spalla	spal-la
skin	la pelle	pel-lay

stomach	lo stomaco	sto-ma-ko
thigh	la coscia	ko-sha
throat	la gola	go-la
thumb	il pollice	pol-lee-chay
toe	il dito	dee-toh
tongue	la lingua	leen-gwa
tonsils	le tonsille	ton-seel-lay
tooth	il dente	den-tay
vein	la vena	ve-na
wrist	il polso	pol-so

At the dentist's

I must see a dentist	Debbo vedere un dentista
Can I make an appointment with the dentist?	Posso fissare un appuntamento col dentista?
As soon as possible	Il più presto possibile
I have toothache	Ho mal di denti
This tooth hurts	Questo dente mi fa male
I've lost a filling	Mi è caduta l'otturazione
Can you fill it?	Può otturarlo?
Can you do it now?	Può farlo adesso?
Must you take the tooth out?	Mi deve togliere il dente?
I do not want the tooth taken out	Non voglio togliermi il dente
Please give me an injection first	Per favore, mi faccia una iniezione prima
My gums are swollen/keep bleeding	Le mie gengive sono gonfie/continuano a sanguinare
I have broken/chipped my dentures	Mi si è rotta/scheggiata la dentiera

Can you fix it (temporarily)?	Può aggiustarla (provvisoriamente)?
You're hurting me	Mi fa male
How much do I owe you?	Quanto Le debbo?
When should I come again?	Quando debbo tornare?
Please rinse your mouth	*Si sciacqui la bocca, per favore
I will X-ray your teeth	*Le faccio la radiografia (ai denti)
You have an abscess	*Ha un ascesso
The nerve is exposed	*Il nervo è esposto
This tooth will have to come out	*Questo dente bisogna toglierlo

Problems and accidents

Where's the police station[1]?	Dov'è il posto di polizia?
Call the police	Chiami la polizia
Where is the British consulate?	Dov'è il consolato britannico?
Please let the consulate know	Informi il consolato, per favore
My bag/wallet has been stolen	Mi hanno rubato la borsa/il portafoglio
I found this in the street	Ho trovato questo per la strada

1. The control of traffic is performed by the *vigili urbani* as well as by *Pubblica Sicurezza* and the *carabinieri*, who are in fact a branch of the army. The *carabinieri* also perform other police duties, and on entering most towns and villages there is a notice which gives the telephone number of the local police under the words *Pronto Intervento*. Most other police work is done by officers of the *Questura*, who combine some of the functions of a district attorney's department and the C.I.D. Both the *vigili* and the *carabinieri* are empowered to give on-the-spot fines, for which they issue a receipt. These are best paid immediately – to dispute them is often time-consuming and comparatively expensive; but the police usually do no more than warn foreign visitors unless the offence is particularly blatant. In the event of an accident call the police. It is essential to get full details of the other driver's insurance, licence and registration.

I have lost my luggage/passport/ travellers' cheques	Ho perso i bagagli/il passaporto/ il blocchetto dei travellers' cheques
I have missed my train	Ho perso il treno
My luggage is on board	I miei bagagli sono a bordo
Call a doctor	Chiami un dottore
Call an ambulance	Chiami un'ambulanza
There has been an accident	C'è stato un incidente
He's badly hurt	E ferito gravemente
He has fainted	E svenuto
He's losing blood	Perde sangue
Please get some water/a blanket/ some bandages	Porti un po' d'acqua/una coperta/della fascie, per favore
I've broken my glasses	Ho rotto gli occhiali
I can't see	Non posso vedere
A child has fallen in the water	Un ragazzo è cascato nell'acqua
First aid, quickly	Il pronto soccorso, subito
May I see your insurance certificate?	Posso vedere il suo certificato d'assicurazione?
Apply to the insurance company	*Si rivolga alla compagnia di assicurazione
I want a copy of the police report	Voglio una copia del verbale di polizia
There's a bus strike	*C'è lo sciopero degli autobus

What are the name and address of the owner?

Quale è il nome e l'indirizzo del proprietario?

Are you willing to act as a witness?

E disposto a far da testimone?

Can I have your name and address, please?

Vuol darmi il Suo nome e indirizzo, per favore?

Can you help me?

Può aiutarmi?

Time and dates

TIME	IL TEMPO
What time is it?	Che ore sono?
It's one o'clock	E l' una
2 o'clock	Sono le due
quarter to ten	Manca un quarto alle dieci/ sono le dieci meno un quarto
twenty to three	Manca venti alle tre/sono le tre meno venti
quarter past five	Sono le cinque e un quarto
half past four	Sono le quattro e mezza
five past eight	Sono le otto e cinque
Second	Il secondo
Minute	Il minuto
Hour	L'ora f
It's early/late	E presto/è tardi

My watch is slow/fast/has stopped	Il mio orologio va indietro/va avanti/è fermo	
Sorry I'm late	Mi scusi per il ritardo	

DATE

LA DATA

What's the date?	Quanti ne abbiamo?
It's 9 December[1]	E il nove dicembre
We got here on 27 July	Siamo arrivati qui il ventisette luglio
We're leaving on 5 January	Partiamo il cinque gennaio

DAY	IL GIORNO	jor-no
Morning	la mattina	mat-tee-na
this morning	stamani	sta-ma-nee
in the morning	di mattina	dee mat-tee-na
Midday, noon	mezzogiorno	med-zo-jor-no
Afternoon	il pomeriggio	po-mair-eej-jo
yesterday afternoon	ieri pomeriggio	yair-ee po-mair-eej-jo
Evening	la sera	se-ra
tomorrow evening	domani sera	do-ma-nee se-ra
Midnight	mezzanotte	med-za-not-tay

1. In Italian cardinal numbers are used for dates except for *first*, for which *primo* is used.

Night	la notte	not-tay
tonight	stanotte	sta-not-tay
Sunrise, dawn	l'alba	al-ba
Sunset	il tramonto	tra-mon-toh
Twilight	il crepuscolo	kre-poos-ko-lo
Today	oggi	oj-jee
Yesterday	ieri	yair-ee
day before yesterday	ieri l'altro/ l'altro ieri	yair-ee lal-troh
Tomorrow	domani	do-ma-nee
day after tomorrow	domani l'altro	do-ma-nee lal-troh
In ten days' time	fra dieci giorni	fra dye-chee jor-nee
WEEK	LA SETTIMANA	set-tee-ma-na
Sunday	domenica	do-me-nee-ka
Monday	lunedì	lee-ne-dee
Tuesday	martedì	mar-te-dee
Wednesday	mercoledì	mer-ko-le-dee
Thursday	giovedì	jo-ve-dee
Friday	venerdì	ven-air-dee
Saturday	sabato	sa-ba-toh
on Tuesday	martedì	mar-te-dee
on Sundays	la domenica	la do-me-nee-ka

Fortnight	quindicina di giorni	kween-dee-chee-na dee jor-nee
MONTH	**IL MESE**	me-se
January	gennaio	jen-na-yo
February	febbraio	feb-bra-yo
March	marzo	mart-zo
April	aprile	a-pree-lay
May	maggio	maj-jo
June	giugno	joon-yo
July	luglio	lool-yo
August	agosto	a-gos-toh
September	settembre	set-tem- bray
October	ottobre	ot-to-bray
November	novembre	no-vem-bray
December	dicembre	dee-chem-bray
SEASON	**LA STAGIONE**	sta-jo-nay
Spring	la primavera	pree-ma-vair-a
Summer	l'estate f	es-ta-tay
Autumn	l'autunno m	ow-toon-no
Winter	l'inverno m	een-vair-no

in spring	a primavera	a pree-ma-vair-a
during the summer	durante l'estate	doo-ran-tay les-ta-tay

YEAR	L'ANNO *m*	an-no
this year	quest'anno	kwest-an-no
next year	l'anno prossimo	an-no pros-see-mo
last year	l'anno scorso	an-no skor-tso

Public holidays

1 January		Capodanno
Easter Monday		Lunedì dell' Angelo
25 April	(Liberation day)	Anniversario della Liberazione
1 May	(Labour day)	Festa del lavoro
15 August	(The Assumption)	Assunzione
1 November	(All Saints' Day)	Tutti i Santi
8 December	(Conception of the Virgin)	Immacolata Concezione
25 December		Natale
26 December		S. Stefano

Local Feast Days are held in honour of the patron saints of various towns, such as:

25 April	(St Mark) in Venice
24 June	(St John the Baptist) in Florence, Genoa and Turin
19 September	(St Gennaro) in Naples
4 October	(St Petronio) in Bologna
7 December	(St Ambrose) in Milan

Numbers

CARDINAL

0	zero	dze-ro
1	uno	oo-no
2	due	doo-ay
3	tre	tray
4	quattro	kwat-troh
5	cinque	cheen-kway
6	sei	se-ee
7	sette	set-tay
8	otto	ot-toh
9	nove	no-vay
10	dieci	dyay-chee
11	undici	**oon**-dee-chee
12	dodici	**do**-dee-chee
13	tredici	**tray**-dee-chee

14	quattordici	**kwat**-tor-dee-chee
15	quindici	**kween**-dee-chee
16	sedici	se-dee-chee
17	diciassette	**dee**-chias-set-tay
18	diciotto	**dee**-chiot-to
19	diciannove	**dee**-chian-no-vay
20	venti	ven-tee
21	ventuno	ven-too-no
22	ventidue	ven-tee-doo-ay
30	trenta	tren-ta
31	trentuno	tren-too-no
40	quaranta	kwa-ran-ta
50	cinquanta	cheen-kwan-ta
60	sessanta	ses-san-ta
70	settanta	set-tan-ta
80	ottanta	ot-tan-ta
90	novanta	no-van-ta
100	cento	chen-toh
101	cento uno	chen-toh oo-no
200	duecento	doo-ay-chen-toh
1,000	mille	meel-lay
2,000	due mila	doo-ay mee-la
1,000,000	un milione	mee-lyo-nay

ORDINAL

1st	primo	pree-mo
2nd	secondo	se-kon-doh
3rd	terzo	tair-tsoh
4th	quarto	kwar-toh
5th	quinto	kween-toh
6th	sesto	ses-toh
7th	settimo	set-tee-mo
8th	ottavo	ot-ta-vo
9th	nono	no-no
10th	decimo	de-chee-mo
11th	undicesimo	oon-dee-che-see-mo
12th	dodicesimo	do-dee-che-see-mo
13th	tredicesimo	tray-dee-che-see-mo
14th	quattordicesimo	kwat-tor-dee-che-see-mo
15th	quindicesimo	kween-dee-che-see-mo
16th	sedicesimo	se-dee-che-see-mo
17th	diciassettesimo	dee-chas-set-te-see-mo
18th	diciottesimo	dee-chot-te-see-mo
19th	diciannovesimo	dee-chan-no-ve-see-mo
20th	ventesimo	ven-te-see-mo
30th	trentesimo	tren-te-see-mo
40th	quarantesimo	kwa-ran-te-see-mo
50th	cinquantesimo	cheen-kwan-te-see-mo

60th	sessantesimo	ses-san-te-see-mo
70th	settantesimo	set-tan-te-see-mo
80th	ottantesimo	ot-tan-te-see-mo
90th	novantesimo	no-van-te-see-mo
100th	centesimo	chen-te-see-mo
half	un mezzo	med-zo
quarter	un quarto	kwar-toh
three quarters	tre quarti	tray kwar-tee
a third	un terzo	ter-tsoh
two thirds	due terzi	doo-ay ter-tsee

Weights and measures

DISTANCE:
kilometres – miles

km.	miles or km.	miles		km.	miles or km.	miles
1·6	1	0·6		14·5	9	5·6
3·2	2	1·2		16·1	10	6·2
4·8	3	1·9		32·2	20	12·4
6·4	4	2·5		40·2	25	15·3
8	5	3·1		80·5	50	31·1
9·7	6	3·7		160·9	100	62·1
11·3	7	4·4		804·7	500	310·7
12·9	8	5·0				

A rough way to convert from miles to km.: divide by 5 and multiply by 8; from km. to miles, divide by 8 and multiply by 5.

LENGTH AND HEIGHT:
centimetres – inches

cm.	*inch or cm.*	inch		cm.	*inch or cm.*	inch
2·5	1	0·4		17·8	7	2·8
5·1	2	0·8		20	8	3·2
7·6	3	1·2		22·9	9	3·5
10·2	4	1·6		25·4	10	3·9
12·7	5	2·0		50·8	20	7·9
15·2	6	2·4		127	50	19·7

A rough way to convert from inches to cm.: divide by 2 and multiply by 5; from cm. to inches, divide by 5 and multiply by 2.

metres – feet

m.	*ft or m.*	ft		m.	*ft or m.*	ft
0·3	1	3·3		2·4	8	26·3
0·6	2	6·6		2·7	9	29·5
0·9	3	9·8		3	10	32·8
1·2	4	13·1		6·1	20	65·6
1·5	5	16·4		15·2	50	164
1·8	6	19·7		30·5	100	328·1
2·1	7	23				

A rough way to convert from ft to m.: divide by 10 and multiply by 3; from m. to ft, divide by 3 and multiply by 10.

metres – yards

m.	yds or m.	yds		m.	yds or m.	yds
0·9	1	1·1		7·3	8	8·8
1·8	2	2·2		8·2	9	9·8
2·7	3	3·3		9·1	10	10·9
3·7	4	4·4		18·3	20	21·9
4·6	5	5·5		45·7	50	54·7
5·5	6	6·6		91·4	100	109·4
6·4	7	7·7		457·2	500	546·8

A rough way to convert from yds to m.: subtract 10 per cent from the number of yds; from m. to yds, add 10 per cent to the number of metres.

LIQUID MEASURES:

litres – gallons

litres	galls. or litres	galls.		litres	galls. or litres	galls.
4·6	1	0·2		36·4	8	1·8
9·1	2	0·4		40·9	9	2·0
13·6	3	0·7		45·5	10	2·2
18·2	4	0·9		90·9	20	4·4
22·7	5	1·1		136·4	30	6·6
27·3	6	1·3		181·8	40	8·8
31·8	7	1·5		227·3	50	11

1 pint = 0·6 litre   1 litre = 1·8 pints.

A rough way to convert from galls. to litres: divide by 2 and multiply by 9; from litres to galls., divide by 9 and multiply by 2.

WEIGHT:
kilogrammes – pounds

kg.	lb. or kg.	lb.		kg.	lb. or kg.	lb.
0·5	1	2·2		3·2	7	15·4
0·9	2	4·4		3·6	8	17·6
1·4	3	6·6		4·1	9	19·8
1·8	4	8·8		4·5	10	22·1
2·3	5	11·0		9·1	20	44·1
2·7	6	13·2		22·7	50	110·2

A rough way to convert from lb. to kg.: divide by 11 and multiply by 5; from kg. to lb., divide by 5 and multiply by 11.

grammes – ounces

grammes	oz.		oz.	grammes
100	3·5		2	57·1
250	8·8		4	114·3
500	17·6		8	228·6
1000 (1 kg.)	35		16 (1 lb.)	457·2

TEMPERATURE

centigrade (°C) – fahrenheit (°F)

°C	°F
—10	14
—5	23
0	32
5	41
10	50
15	59
20	68
25	77
30	86
35	95
37	98·4
38	100·5
39	102
40	104
100	180

To convert °F to °C: deduct 32, divide by 9, multiply by 5; to convert °C to °F: divide by 5, multiply by 9, and add 32.

Vocabulary

Various groups of specialized words are given elsewhere in this book and these words are usually not repeated in the Vocabulary:

A

a, an	un, una	oon, oo-na
able (to be)	potere	po-tair-ay
about	circa	cheer-ka
above	sopra	so-pra
abroad	all'estero	al-les-tair-oh
accept (to)	accettare	a-chet-tar-ay
accident	l'incidente *m*	een-chee-den-tay
ache (to)	dolere	do-le-ray
acquaintance	il conoscente	kon-oh-shen-tay
across	attraverso	at-tra-vair-so
act (to)	agire	a-jee-ray
add (to)	aggiungere	aj-**joon**-jair-ray
address	l'indirizzo *m*	een-dee-reet-so
admire (to)	ammirare	am-mee-ra-ray
admission	l'ingresso *m*/ l'entrata *f*	een-gres-so/ en-tra-ta
advice	il consiglio	kon-seel-yo
aeroplane	l'aeroplano *m*	a-air-oh-plah-no
afraid (to be)	(aver) paura	(a-vair) pow-ra
after	dopo	doh-po
again	ancora	ang-kor-a
against	contro	kon-troh

age	l'età *f*	**ay-ta**
ago	(tempo) fa	(tem-po) fa
agree (to)	essere d'accordo	es-sair-ay dak-or-doh
air	l'aria *f*	**ar-ee-a**
air-conditioning	il condizionatore (d'aria)	kon-deets-yon-a-tor-ay (**dar-ee-a**)
all	tutto	toot-toh
all right	va bene	va bay-nay
allow (to)	permettere	pair-met-tair-ray
almost	quasi	kwa-zee
alone	solo	so-lo
along	lungo	loon-go
already	già	ja
also	anche	an-kay
alter (to)	modificare	mo-dee-fee-kar-ray
alternative	l'alternativa *f*	al-tair-na-tee-va
although	benchè	ben-**kay**
always	sempre	sem-pray
ambulance	l'ambulanza *f*	am-boo-lant-sa
America	America *f*	a-**me**-ree-ka
American	americano	a-me-ree-**ka**-no
amuse (to)	divertire	dee-vair-teer-ay
amusing	divertente	dee-vair-ten-tay
ancient	vecchio	vek-yo

and	e	ay
angry	arrabbiato	ar-rab-bya-toh
animal	l'animale *m*	a-nee-ma-lay
anniversary	l'anniversario	an-nee-vair-sa-ree-oh
annoyed	seccato	sek-ka-toh
another	un altro	oon al-troh
answer	la risposta	rees-pos-ta
answer (to)	rispondere	rees-**pon**-deh-ray
antique	antico	an-tee-ko
any	qualche/qualunque	kwal-kay/kwal-oon-kway
anyone	qualcuno/chiunque	kwal-koo-no/kee-oon-kway
anything	qualchecosa	kwal-kay-koh-za
anywhere	dovunque	doh-voon-kway
apartment	l'appartamento *m*	ap-par-ta-men-toh
apologize (to)	scusarsi	skoo-zar-see
appetite	l'appetito *m*	ap-pet-ee-toh
appointment	l'appuntamento *m*	ap-poon-ta-men-toh
architect	l'architetto *m*	ar-kee-tet-toh
architecture	l'architettura *f*	ar-kee-tet-too-ra
area	la zona/la regione	tso-na/re-jo-nay
arm	il braccio	brach-yo
armchair	la poltrona	pol-troh-na

army	l'esercito m	e-ser-chee-toh
arrange (to)	combinare	kom-bee-na-ray
arrival	l'arrivo m	ar-ree-vo
arrive (to)	arrivare	ar-ree-va-ray
art	l'arte f	ar-tay
art gallery	la galleria d'arte	gal-lair-ee-a dar-tay
artist	l'artista	ar-tees-ta
as	come	ko-may
as much as	tanto quanto	tan-toh kwan-toh
as soon as	appena che	ap-pain-a kay
as well	in più/come pure	een pyoo/ko-may poo-ray
ashtray	il portacenere	por-ta-che-nair-ay
ask (to)	chiedere	kee-e-dair-ay
asleep	addormentato	ad-dor-men-ta-toh
at	a	a
at last	finalmente	fee-nal-men-tay
at once	subito	soo-bee-toh
atmosphere	l'atmosfera f	at-mos-fair-a
attention	l'attenzione f	at-tents-yoh-nay
attractive	attraente	at-tra-en-tay
auction	l'asta	as-ta
audience	l'uditorio m	oo-dee-tor-yo
aunt	la zia	tsee-a

Australia	Australia *f*	ow-stra-lee-a
Australian	australiano	ow-stra-lya-no
author	l'autore *m*	ow-tor-ray
available	disponibile	dees-poh-nee-blay
average	la media	med-ya
awake	sveglio	zvay-lyo
away	via	vee-a

B

baby	il bambino	bam-bee-no
bachelor	il celibe	che-lee-bay
back *adv.*	indietro	een-dyay-troh
bad	cattivo	kat-tee-vo
bad *food*	guasto	gwas-toh
bag	la borsa	bor-sa
baggage	i bagagli	ba-ga-lyee
bait	lo spuntino	spoon-tee-no
balcony	il balcone	bal-koh-nay
ball *sport*	la palla	pal-la
ballet	il balletto	bal-let-toh
band *music*	l'orchestra *f*	or-kes-tra
bank	la banca	bang-ka
basket	il cesto	ches-toh

bath	il bagno	ban-yoh
bathe (to)	fare un bagno	fa-ray oon ban-yo
bathing cap	la cuffia da bagno	koof-fya da ban-yo
bathing costume	il costume da bagno	kos-too-may da ban-yo
bathing trunks	i calzoncini da bagno	kalt-son-chee-nee da ban-yo
bathroom	la stanza da bagno	stant-sa da ban-yo
battery	la batteria	bat-tair-ee-a
bay *sea*	la baia	by-ya
be (to)	essere	es-sair-ay
beach	la spiaggia	spee-aj-ja
beard	la barba	bar-ba
beautiful	bello	bel-lo
because	perchè	pair-**kay**
become (to)	divenire	de-ve-nee-ray
bed	il letto	let-toh
bedroom	la camera	**ka**-mair-a
before *space*	davanti a	da-van-tee a
time	prima di	pree-ma dee
begin (to)	cominciare	ko-meen-char-ay
beginning	il principio	preen-cheep-yo
behind	dietro	dee-ay-troh
believe (to)	credere	**kred**-air-ay
bell	il campanello	kam-pa-nel-lo

belong (to)	appartenere	ap-par-ten-air-ay
below	sotto	sot-oh
belt	la cintura	cheen-too-ra
bench	la panchina	pan-chee-na
bend	la curva	koor-vay
berth	il letto	let-toh
best	il migliore	meel-yor-ray
bet	la scommessa	skom-mes-sa
better	meglio/migliore	mel-yoh/meel-yor-ray
between	fra	fra
bicycle	la bicicletta	bee-chee-kle-ta
big	grande	gran-day
bill	il conto	kon-toh
binoculars	il binocolo	bee-no-ko-lo
bird	l'uccello *m*	oo-chel-lo
birthday	il compleanno	kom-play-an-no
bite (to)	mordere	mor-dair-ay
bitter	amaro	a-ma-ro
blanket	la coperta	ko-pair-ta
bleach (to)	ossigenare	os-see-jen-ar-ray
bleed (to)	sanguinare	san-gwee-nar-ray
blind	cieco	chee-e-ko
blood	il sangue	san-gway
blouse	la blusa	bloo-za

blow *hit*	il colpo	kol-po
blow (to)	soffiare	sof-fee-a-ray
(on) board	a bordo	a bor-doh
boarding house	la pensione	pens-yo-nay
boat	il battello	bat-tel-lo
body	il corpo	kor-poh
bone	l'osso *m*	os-so
bonfire	il falò	fa-lo
book	il libro	lee-bro
book (to)	riservare	ree-zair-va-ray
boot *for foot*	lo stivale	stee-va-lay
border	la frontiera/ il confine	front-yair-a/ kon-fee-nay
borrow (to)	prendere in prestito	pren-dair-ay een pres-tee-toh
both	entrambi	en-tram-bee
bottle	la bottiglia	bot-teel-ya
bottle opener	il cavatappi	ka-va-tap-pee
bottom	il fondo	fon-doh
bowl	la tazza	tat-sa
box *container*	la scatola	ska-toh-la
theatre	il palco	pal-koh
box office	il botteghino	bot-te-ghee-no
boy	il ragazzo	ra-gat-zo

bracelet	il braccialetto	bra-cha-let-toh
braces	le bretelle	bre-tel-lay
brain	il cervello	chair-vel-lo
brains	le cervella	chair-vel-la
branch *tree*	il ramo	ra-mo
office	la filiale/	feel-ya-lay/
	la succursale	sook-koor-sa-lay
brassière	il reggiseno	red-jee-se-no
break (to)	rompere	**rom**-pair-ay
breakfast	la prima colazione	pree-ma
		ko-latz-yo-nay
breathe (to)	respirare	res-peer-ar-ay
bridge	il ponte	pon-tay
briefs *women's*	le mutandine per	moo-tan-dee-nay pair
	donna	don-na
bright *light*	lucente	loo-chen-tay
bring (to)	portare	por-tar-ray
British	britannico	bree-**tan**-nee-ko
broken	rotto	rot-toh
brooch	la spilla	speel-la
brother	il fratello	fra-tel-lo
bruise (to)	ammaccarsi	am-mak-kar-see
brush	la spazzola	spat-so-la
brush (to)	spazzolare	spat-so-la-ray

bucket	la secchia	sek-kya
buckle	la fibbia	feeb-bya
build (to)	costruire	kos-troo-eer-ay
building	l'edificio *m*	ed-ee-fee-cho
bunch *flowers, keys*	il mazzo	mad-zo
buoy	la boa	boh-a
burn (to)	bruciare	broo-char-ray
burst (to)	scoppiare	skop-pyar-ray
bus	l'autobus *m*	ow-toh-boos
bus stop	la fermata d'autobus	fair-ma-ta
business	gli affari	af-far-ee
busy	occupato	ok-koo-pa-toh
but	ma	ma
button	il bottone	bot-toh-nay
buy (to)	comprare	kom-prar-ay

C

cab	il tassì	tas-see
cabin	la cabina	ka-bee-na
call *telephone*	la chiamata	kee-am-a-ta
call (to) *summon*	chiamare	kee-am-ar-ay
visit	visitare	vee-zee-tar-ay
calm	calmo	kal-mo

camp (to)	accamparsi	ak-kam-par-see
camp site	posto per campeggio	pos-toh pair kam-ped-jo
can (to be able)	potere	po-tair-ay
can *tin*	il barattolo	ba-rat-toh-lo
Canada	Canadà *m*	ka-na-**da**
Canadian	canadese	ka-na-day-say
cancel (to)	cancellare	kan-chel-la-**ra**
candle	la candela	kan-de-la
canoe	la canoa	ka-no-a
cap	il berretto	ber-ret-toh
capital city	la capitale	ka-pee-ta-lay
car	la macchina	**ma**-kee-na
car park	il parcheggio	par-ked-jo
caravan	la roulotte	roo-lot
care	la cura	koo-ra
careful	attento	at-ten-toh
careless	disordinato	dee-sor-dee-na-toh
carry (to)	portare	por-ta-ray
cash	la cassa i contanti	kas-sa ee kon-tan-tee
cash (to)	incassare	een-kas-sar-ay
cashier	il cassiere	kas-syair-ay
casino	il casinò	ka-zee-**no**
castle	il castello	kas-tel-lo

cat	il gatto	gat-toh
catalogue	il catalogo	ka-ta-loh-go
catch (to)	prendere	pren-dair-ay
cathedral	la cattedrale/ il duomo	kat-tay-dra-lay/ dwo-mo
catholic	cattolico	kat-tol-lee-ko
cave	la grotta	grot-ta
centre	il centro	chen-troh
central	centrale	chen-tra-lay
century	il secolo	se-koh-lo
ceremony	la cerimonia	cher-ree-mon-ya
certain(ly)	certo	chair-toh
chair	la sedia	sed-ya
chambermaid	la cameriera	ka-mair-yair-ah
chance	il caso	ka-so
(small) change	gli spiccioli	spee-chol-ee
change (to)	cambiare	kam-byar-ay
charge *money*	il costo	kos-toh
money	far pagare	far pa-gar-ay
cheap	a buon mercato	a bwon mair-ka-toh
check (to)	controllare	kon-trol-lar-ay
cheque	l'assegno *m*	as-sen-yo
child	il bambino	bam-bee-no
china	la porcellana	por-chel-la-na

choice	la scelta	shel-ta
choose (to)	scegliere	shel-yair-ay
church	la chiesa	kee-e-za
cigarette case	il portasigarette	por-ta-see-ga-ret-tay
cinema	il cinema	chee-ne-ma
circle *theatre*	la galleria	gal-lair-ee-a
circus	il circo	cheer-ko
city	la città	cheet-ta
class	la classe	klas-say
clean	pulito	poo-lee-toh
clean (to)	pulire	poo-lee-ray
clear	chiaro	kee-a-ro
cliff	la scogliera	skol-yair-a
climb (to)	arrampicarsi	a-ram-pee-kar-see
cloakroom	il guardaroba	gwar-da-roh-ba
clock	l'orologio *m*	or-oh-lo-jo
close (to)	chiudere	kyoo-de-ray
closed	chiuso	kyoo-so
cloth	la stoffa	stof-fa
clothes	i vestiti	ves-tee-tee
cloud	la nube	noo-bay
coach	il pullman	pool-man
coast	la costa	kos-ta
coat	il soprabito	sop-ra-bee-toh

coathanger	l'attaccapanni *m*	a-ta-ka-pan-nee
coin	la moneta	mo-nay-ta
cold	freddo	fred-doh
collar	il colletto	kol-let-oh
collar stud	il bottoncino da colletto	bot-ton-chee-no da kol-let-toh
collect (to)	raccogliere	re-kol-ye-ray
colour	il colore	ko-lor-ay
comb	il pettine	pet-tee-nay
come (to)	venire	ve-nee-ray
come in	entrate	en-tra-tay
comfortable	comodo	ko-moh-doh
company	la compagnia	kom-pan-yee-a
compartment *train*	lo scompartimento	scom-par-tee-men-toh
complain (to)	lagnarsi	lan-yar-see
complaint	la lagnanza	lan-yan-tsa
complete	completo	kom-play-toh
concert	il concerto	kon-chair-toh
condition	la condizione	kon-dee-tsyo-nay
conductor *bus*	il fattorino	fat-tor-ee-no
orchestra	il direttore	dee-ret-tor-ray
congratulations	congratulazioni	kon-gra-too-lats-yo-nee
connect (to)	connettere	kon-net-te-ray

connection *train, etc.*	la coincidenza	ko-een-chee-dent-sa
consul	il console	**kon**-so-lay
consulate	il consolato	kon-so-la-toh
contain (to)	contenere	kon-ten-air-ay
contrast	il contrasto	kon-tras-toh
convenient	conveniente	kon-ven-yen-tay
convent	il convento	kon-ven-toh
conversation	la conversazione	kon-vair-sats-yo-nay
cook	il cuoco	kwo-ko
cook (to)	cucinare	koo-chee-nar-ay
cool	fresco	fres-ko
copper	il rame	ra-may
copy	la copia	ko-pya
copy (to)	copiare	ko-pya-ray
cork	il tappo	tap-poh
corkscrew	il cavatappi	ka-va-tap-pee
corner	l'angolo *m*	**an**-go-lo
correct	corretto	kor-ret-toh
corridor	il corridoio	kor-ree-doh-yo
cosmetics	i cosmetici	kos-me-tee-chee
cost	il costo	kos-toh
cost (to)	costare	kos-tar-ay
cottage	la casetta di campagna	ka-set-ta dee kam-pan-ya

cotton	il cotone	ko-toh-nay
cotton wool	l'ovatta *f*	oh-vat-ta
couchette	la cuccetta	koo-chet-ta
count (to)	contare	kon-tar-ay
country *nation*	il paese	pa-ay-zay
not town	la campagna	kam-pan-ya
course *dish*	la portata	por-ta-ta
cousin	il cugino	koo-jee-no
cover charge	il coperto	ko-pair-toh
cross	la croce	kro-chay
cross (to)	attraversare	at-tra-vair-sa-ray
crossroads	il crocevia	kro-chay-vee-a
cufflinks	i gemelli	jem-el-lee
cup	la tazza	tat-sah
cupboard	l'armadio *m*	ar-mad-yo
cure (to)	guarire	gwa-reer-ay
curious	curioso	koo-ree-o-so
curl	il riccio	ree-choh
current	la corrente	kor-ren-tay
curtain	la tenda	ten-da
cushion	il cuscino	koo-shee-no
customs	la dogana	do-ga-na
customs officer	l'ufficiale di dogana *m*	oof-fee-cha-lay dee do-ga-na

| cut | il taglio | tal-yo |
| cut (to) | tagliare | tal-yar-ay |

D

daily	quotidiano	kwot-eed-ya-no
damaged	danneggiato	dan-ned-ja-toh
damp	umido	oo-mee-doh
dance	il ballo	bal-lo
dance (to)	ballare	bal-lar-ay
danger	pericolo	pe-ree-ko-lo
dangerous	pericoloso	pe-ree-ko-lo-so
dark	scuro	skoo-ro
date *appointment*	l'appuntamento *m*	ap-poon-ta-men-toh
calendar	la data	da-ta
daughter	la figlia	feel-ya
day	il giorno	jor-no
dead	morto	mor-toh
deaf	sordo	sor-doh
dear	caro	kar-ro
decide (to)	decidere	de-chee-de-ray
deckchair	la sedia a sdraio	sed-ya a zdra-yo
declare (to)	dichiarare	dee-kyar-ar-ay
deep	profondo	pro-fon-doh

delay	il ritardo	ree-tar-doh
deliver (to)	consegnare	kon-sen-yar-ay
delivery	la consegna	kon-sen-ya
demi-pension	la mezza pensione	med-za pens-yo-nay
dentist	il dentista	den-tees-ta
dentures	la dentiera	dent-yair-a
deodorant	il deodorante	de-oh-dor-an-tay
depart (to)	partire	par-tee-ray
department	il dipartimento	dee-par-tee-men-toh
department stores	i grandi magazzini	gran-dee ma-ga-dzee-nee
departure	la partenza	par-tent-sa
dessert	il dessert	des-sairt
detour	la deviazione	day-vee-ats-yo-nay
dial (to)	comporre il numero	kom-po-ray eel noo-me-ro
diamond	il diamante	dee-a-man-tay
dice	i dadi	da-dee
dictionary	il dizionario	deets-yon-ar-yo
diet	la dieta	dee-ay-ta
diet (to)	stare a dieta	sta-ray a dee-ay-ta
different	differente	deef-fair-en-tay
difficult	difficile	deef-fee-chee-lay
dine (to)	pranzare	pran-za-ray

dining room	la sala da pranzo	sa-la da pran-zo
dinner	il pranzo	pran-zo
direct	diretto	dee-re-toh
direction	la direzione	dee-rets-yo-nay
dirty	sporco	spor-ko
disappointed	deluso	de-loo-so
discothèque	la discoteca	dees-ko-te-ka
dish	il piatto	pee-at-toh
disinfectant	il disinfettante	dees-een-fet-tan-tay
distance	la distanza	dees-tant-sa
disturb (to)	disturbare	dees-toor-bar-ay
ditch	il fosso	fos-so
dive (to)	tuffarsi	toof-far-see
diving board	il trampolino di lancio	tram-po-lee-no dee lan-cho
divorced	divorziato	dee-vort-see-a-toh
do (to)	fare	fa-ray
dock (to)	attraccare	at-trak-kar-ay
doctor	il dottore	dot-tor-ay
dog	il cane	ka-nay
doll	la bambola	bam-boh-la
door	la porta	por-ta
double	doppio	dop-pyo

double bed	il letto matrimoniale	let-toh ma-tree-mon-ya-lay
double room	la camera matrimoniale	ka-mair-a ma-tree-mon-ya-lay
down (stairs)	giù	joo
dozen	la dozzina	dod-zee-na
drawer	il cassetto	kas-set-toh
dream	il sogno	son-yo
dress	l'abito *m*	a-bee-toh
dressing gown	la vestaglia	ves-tal-ya
dressmaker	il sarto	sar-toh
drink (to)	bere	ber-ay
drinking water	acqua potabile	ak-wa po-ta-bee-lay
drive (to)	guidare	gwee-da-ray
driver	il conduttore	kon-doot-tor-ray
drop (to)	cadere	ka-de-ray
drunk	ubriaco	oo-bree-a-cho
dry	secco, asciutto	sek-koh, ash-ot-toh
during	durante	doo-ran-tay

E

| each | ciascuno | chas-koo-no |
| early | di buon' ora | dee bwon or-a |

earrings	gli orecchini	or-rek-ee-nee
east	est *m*	est
easy	facile	**fa**-chee-lay
eat (to)	mangiare	man-jar-ay
edge	la sponda	spon-da
eiderdown	il piumino	pyoo-mee-no
elastic	l'elastico *m*	e-**las**-tee-ko
electric light bulb	la lampadina	lam-pa-dee-na
electric point	la presa elettrica	pre-sa el-et-tree-ka
electricity	l'elettricità	el-et-ree-chee-**ta**
elevator	l'ascensore *m*	ash-en-sor-ay
embarrassed	imbarazzato	eem-ba-rad-za-toh
embassy	l'ambasciata *f*	am-ba-sha-ta
emergency exit	l'uscita di sicurezza *f*	oo-shee-ta dee see-koo-ret-sa
empty	vuoto	vwo-toh
end	la fine	fee-nay
engaged *people*	fidanzato	fee-dant-sa-toh
busy	occupato	ok-koo-pa-toh
engine	il motore	mo-tor-ay
England	Inghilterra *f*	eeng-eel-ter-ra
English	inglese	eeng-lay-zay
enjoy (to)	godere	go-de-ray
enjoy oneself (to)	divertirsi	dee-ver-teer-see

enough	abbastanza	ab-bas-tant-sa
enquiries	informazioni	een-for-mats-yo-nee
enter (to)	entrare	en-tra-ray
entrance	l'ingresso *m*	een-gres-so
envelope	la busta	boos-ta
equipment	l'attrezzatura *f*	att-ret-sa-too-ra
escape (to)	scappare	skap-pa-ray
Europe	Europa *f*	ay-oo-ro-pa
even *not odd*	pari	pa-ree
event	l'evento *m*	e-ven-toh
every	ogni	on-yee
everybody	ognuno	on-yoo-no
everything	tutto	toot-toh
everywhere	dovunque	doh-voon-kway
example	l'esempio *m*	ez-emp-yo
excellent	eccellente	e-chel-len-tay
except	eccetto	e-che-toh
excess	l'eccesso *m*	e-che-so
exchange (bureau)	il cambio	kamb-yo
exchange rate	il cambio	kamb-yo
excursion	la gita	jee-ta
excuse (to)	scusare	skoo-za-ray
exhibition	l'esposizione *f*	es-po-zeets-yo-nay
exit	l'uscita *f*	oo-shee-ta

expect (to)	aspettare	as-pet-tar-ay
expensive	costoso	kos-toh-so
express *letter*	lettera/espresso	let-tair-a/es-pres-so
express train	il rapido	**rap**-ee-doh
extra	extra, in più	es-tra/een pyoo
eye shadow	l'ombretto *m*	om-bret-toh

F

fabric	il tessuto	tes-soo-toh
face	la faccia	fach-ya
fact	il fatto	fat-toh
factory	la fabbrica	**fab**-bree-ka
fade (to)	scolorire	sko-lo-ree-ray
faint (to)	svenire	sven-eer-ay
fair *colour*	chiaro	kee-ar-oh
fête	la fiera	fyair-a
fall (to)	cadere	ka-dair-ay
family	la famiglia	fa-meel-ya
far	lontano	lon-ta-no
fare	il prezzo (del biglietto	pret-zo
farm	la fattoria	fat-tor-ee-a
farmer	l'agricoltore *m*	ag-ree-kol-to-ray

farther	più lontano	pyoo lon-ta-no
fashion	la moda	moh-da
fast	veloce	ve-lo-chay
fat	grasso	gras-so
father	il padre	pa-dray
fault	lo sbaglio	zbal-yo
fear	la paura	pa-oo-ra
feed (to)	alimentare	a-lee-men-ta-ray
feel (to)	sentire	sen-teer-ay
female *adj.*	femminile	fe-mee-nee-lay
ferry	il traghetto	tra-get-toh
fetch (to)	andare a prendere	an-dar-ay a pren-dair-ay
fever	la febbre	feb-bray
a few	alcuni	al-koo-nee
fiancé(e)	il fidanzato/ la fidanzata	fee-dant-za-toh/ fee-dant-za-ta
field	il campo	kam-po
fight (to)	combattere	kom-bat-te-ray
fill (to)	riempire	ree-em-peer-ay
film	il film/ la pellicola	feelm/ pell-ee-ko-la
find (to)	trovare	tro-var-ay
fine *money*	la multa	mool-ta
finish (to)	finire	fee-neer-ay

finished	finito	fee-nee-toh
fire	il fuoco	fwo-ko
fire escape	l'uscita di sicurezza	oo-shee-ta dee see-koo-red-za
first	primo	pree-mo
first aid	il pronto soccorso	pron-toh sok-kor-so
first class	la prima classe	pree-ma kla-say
fish	il pesce	pesh-ay
fish (to)	pescare	pes-kar-ay
fisherman	il pescatore	pes-kat-or-ay
fit (to)	star bene	starr bay-nay
flag	la bandiera	band-yair-a
flat *adj.*	piatto	pya-toh
noun	l'appartamento *m*	ap-par-ta-men-toh
flight	il volo	vo-lo
flood	l'inondazione *f*	een-on-dats-yo-nay
floor *ground*	il pavimento	pa-vee-men-toh
storey	il piano	pee-a-no
floorshow	il cabaret	ka-ba-ray
flower	il fiore	fee-or-ay
fly	la mosca	mos-ka
fly (to)	volare	vo-lar-ay
fog	la nebbia	neb-bya
fold (to)	piegare	pee-e-ga-ray

follow (to)	seguire	seg-weer-ay
food	il cibo	chee-bo
foot	il piede	pee-e-day
football	il calcio	kal-chyo
footpath	il sentiero	sent-yair-oh
for	per	pair
foreign	straniero	stra-nye-ro
forest	la foresta	for-es-ta
forget (to)	dimenticare	dee-men-tee-kar-ay
fork	la forchetta	for-ket-ta
forward	avanti	a-van-tee
forward (to)	inoltrare	een-ol-trar-ay
fountain	la fontana	fon-ta-na
fragile	fragile	fra-jee-lay
free	libero	lee-bair-oh
freight	il nolo	no-lo
fresh	fresco	fres-koh
fresh water	acqua dolce	ak-wa dol-chay
friend	l'amico *m*/l'amica *f*	a-mee-koh/a-mee-ka
friendly	amichevole	a-mee-ke-vo-lay
from	da	da
front	il fronte	fron-tay
frontier	la frontiera	fron-tee-air-a
frozen	congelato	kon-jel-a-toh

fruit	il frutto	froo-toh
full	pieno	pee-en-oh
full board	la pensione completa	pens-yo-nay kom-ple-ta
fun	il divertimento	dee-ver-tee-men-toh
funny	divertente	dee-vair-ten-tay
fur	la pelliccia	pel-lee-chee-a
furniture	il mobilio	mo-bee-lyo

G

gallery	la galleria	gal-lair-ee-a
gamble (to)	giocare d'azzardo	jo-kar-ay dat-zar-doh
game	il giuoco	joo-oh-koh
garage	il garage	ga-ra-jay
garbage	i rifiuti	ree-fyoo-tee
garden	il giardino	jar-dee-noh
gas	il gas	gas
gate	il cancello	kan-chel-lo
gentlemen	Signori, Uomini	seen-yor-ee, wo-mee-nee
get (to)	ottenere	ot-ten-air-ay
get off (to)	scendere	shen-dair-ay
get on (to)	salire	sal-eer-ay
get up (to)	alzarsi	al-tsar-see

gift	il regalo	ray-ga-loh
girdle	il busto	boos-toh
girl	la ragazza	ra-gatz-a
give (to)	dare	da-ray
glad	contento	kon-ten-toh
glass	il bicchiere	bik-yair-ay
glasses	gli occhiali	ok-ya-lee
gloomy	oscuro	os-koo-ro
glove	il guanto	gwan-toh
go (to)	andare	an-dar-ay
god	dio *m*	dee-oh
gold	l'oro *m*	or-oh
good	buono	bwon-oh
government	il governo	gov-air-noh
granddaughter	la nepote	nee-pot-ay
grandfather	il nonno	non-noh
grandmother	la nonna	non-na
grandson	il nepote	nee-pot-ay
grass	l'erba *f*	air-ba
grateful	grato	gra-toh
great	grande	gran-day
ground	il terreno/la terra	ter-re-no/ter-ra
grow (to)	crescere	kre-she-ray
guarantee	la garanzia	gar-ant-see-a

guard	la guardia	gwar-dya
guest	l'ospite *m, f*	os-pee-tay
guide	la guida	gwee-da
guide book	la guida	gwee-da

H

hair	i capelli	kap-el-lee
hair brush	la spazzola da capelli	spat-soh-la da kap-ell-ee
hairpin	la forcina	for-chee-na
half	mezzo	med-zoh
half board	la mezza pensione	med-za pens-yo-nay
half fare	metà prezzo *m*	me-ta pret-zo
hammer	il martello	mar-tel-lo
hand	la mano	ma-no
handbag	la borsetta	bor-set-ta
handkerchief	il fazzoletto	fat-zoh-let-oh
hang (to)	attaccare/ appendere	at-tak-ka-ray/ ap-pen-de-ray
hanger	l'attaccapanni *m*	at-tak-a-pan-nee
happen (to)	accadere	ak-ad-air-ay
happy	felice	fel-ee-chay
happy birthday	buon compleanno	bwon kom-ple-an-no

harbour	il porto	por-toh
hard	duro	doo-ro
hat	il cappello	kap-pel-lo
have (to)	avere	a-vair-ay
he	egli, lui	el-yee, loo-ee
head	la testa	tes-ta
health	la salute	sal-oo-tay
hear (to)	sentire	sen-teer-ay
heart	il cuore	kwor-ay
heat	il calore	kal-or-ay
heating	il riscaldamento	rees-kal-da-men-toh
heavy	pesante	pez-an-tay
heel *shoe*	il tacco	tak-oh
help	l'aiuto *m*	a-yoo-toh
help (to)	aiutare	a-yoo-tar-ay
hem	l'orlo *m*	or-lo
her *adj.*	suo	soo-oh
pron.	le, lei	lay, le-ee
here	qui	kwee
high	alto	al-toh
hike (to)	fare un'escursione a piedi	fa-ray oon-es-koor-syo-nay a pye-dee
hill	la collina	kol-lee-na

him	lui	loo-ee
hire (to)	noleggiare	no-lej-jar-ay
his	suo	soo-oh
hitch hike (to)	fare l'autostop	fa-ray low-toh-stop
hold (to)	tenere	te-ne-ray
hole	il buco	boo-ko
holiday	la vacanza	va-kan-tsa
hollow	vuoto/concavo	vwo-toh/kon-ka-vo
(at) home	a casa	a ka-sa
honeymoon	la luna di miele	loo-na dee mye-lay
hope	la speranza	spe-ran-tsa
hope (to)	sperare	spe-ra-ray
horse	il cavallo	ka-val-lo
horse races	le corse di cavalli	kor-say dee ka-val-lee
horse riding	l'equitazione	e-kwee-ta-tsyo-nay
hospital	l'ospedale *m*	os-pe-da-lay
host/hostess	l'ospite *m/f*	os-pee-tay
hot	caldo	kal-doh
hot water bottle	la borsa d'acqua calda	bor-sa dak-wa kal-da
hotel	l'albergo *m*	al-bair-go
hotel keeper	l'albergatore *m*	al-bair-ga-tor-ay
hour	l'ora *f*	or-a
house	la casa	ka-sa
how?	come?	koh-may

how much/many?	quanto/quanti?	kwan-toh/kwan-tee
hungry (to be)	aver fame	a-**vairr** fa-may
hurry (to)	affrettarsi	af-fret-tar-see
hurt (to)	far male	far may-lay
husband	il marito	ma-ree-toh

I

I	io	ee-oh
if	se	say
immediately	subito	**soo**-bee-toh
important	importante	eem-por-tan-tay
in	in, a	een, a
include (to)	includere	een-kloo-dair-ay
included	compreso	kom-prai-zo
inconvenient	scomodo	**skoh**-mo-do
incorrect	scorretto	skor-ret-toh
indoors	in casa	een ka-sa
information	l'informazione *f*	een-for-mats-yo-nay
ink	l'inchiostro *m*	eenk-yos-tro
inn	l'osteria *f*	os-tair-ee-a
insect	l'insetto *m*	een-set-toh
insect bite	la puntura d'insetto	poon-too-ra deen-set-toh

insect repellent	la lozione anti-insetti	loh-tsyo-nay an-tee een-set-tee
inside	dentro	den-troh
instead	invece	een-vay-chay
instructor	l'istruttore *m*	ees-troot-to-ray
insurance	l'assicurazione *f*	as-see-koo-rats-yo-nay
insure (to)	assicurarsi	as-see-koo-rar-see
interested	interessato	een-tair-es-sa-toh
interesting	interessante	een-tair-es-san-tay
interpreter	l'interprete *m*	een-tair-pre-tay
into	in, dentro	een, den-tro
introduce (to)	presentare	pre-zen-tar-ay
invitation	l'invito *m*	een-vee-toh
invite (to)	invitare	een-vee-tar-ay
Ireland	Irlanda *f*	eer-lan-da
Irish	irlandese	eer-lan-day-zay
iron (to)	stirare	steer-ar-ay
island	l'isola *f*	ee-zoh-la
it	lo	loh
Italian	italiano	ee-tal-ya-no
Italy	Italia *f*	ee-tal-ya

J

jacket	la giacchetta	jak-et-ta
jar	la brocca	brok-ka
jelly fish	la medusa	me-doo-za
jewellery	la gioielleria	joy-el-lair-ee-a
job	il lavoro	la-vo-ro
journey	il viaggio	vee-adj-yo
jump (to)	saltare	sal-ta-ray
jumper	il maglione	mal-yoh-nay

K

keep (to)	tenere	ten-air-ay
key	la chiave	kee-a-vay
kick (to)	dare calci a	da-ray kal-chee a
kind	gentile	jen-tee-lay
king	il re	ray
kiss	il bacio	ba-cho
kiss (to)	baciare	ba-cha-ray
kitchen	la cucina	koo-chee-na
knee	il ginocchio	jee-nok-yoh
knickers	le mutandine per donna	moo-tan-dee-nay pair don-na

knife	il coltello	kol-tel-loh
knock (to)	bussare	boos-sa-ray
know (to) *fact*	sapere	sa-pair-ay
person	conoscere	kon-osh-air-ay

l

label	l'etichetta *f*	et-ee-ket-ta
lace	il merletto	mair-let-toh
ladies	Signore/Donne	seen-yor-ay/don-nay
lake	il lago	la-go
lamp	la lampada	lam-pa-da
land	la terra	ter-ra
landing *plane*	l'atterraggio *m*	at-ter-ra-jo
stairs	il pianerottolo	pee-a-ne-rot-to-lo
landlord	il padrone	pad-roh-nay
lane	il vicolo	vee-ko-loh
language	la lingua	leen-gwa
large	grande	gran-day
last	ultimo	ool-tee-mo
late	tardi	tar-dee
laugh (to)	ridere	ree-dair-ay
lavatory	il gabinetto/	ga-bee-net-toh/
	la toilette	to-eel-et-tay

lavatory paper	la carta igienica	kar-tah eej-yen-ee-ka
law	la legge	lej-jay
lead (to)	condurre	kon-door-ray
leaf	la foglia	fol-ya
leak (to)	perdere	per-day-ray
learn (to)	imparare	eem-par-ar-ay
least *adj.*	minimo	mee-nee-mo
at least	almeno	al-me-no
leather	la pelle	pel-lay
leave (to) *abandon*	lasciare	lash-ar-ay
go away	partire	par-teer-ay
left *opp. right*	sinistro	see-nees-troh
left luggage	il deposito bagagli	de-poz-ee-toh bag-al-yee
leg	la gamba	gam-ba
lend (to)	prestare	press-tar-ay
length	la lunghezza	loon-get-za
less	meno	me-noh
lesson	la lezione	let-syo-nay
let (to) *allow*	permettere	pair-met-tair-ay
rent	affittare	af-fee-ta-ray
letter	la lettera	let-tair-a
level crossing	il passaggio a livello	pa-sa-jo a lee-vel-lo
library	la biblioteca	bee-blee-oh-tek-a

licence	la patente	pa-ten-tay
life	la vita	vee-ta
lift	l'ascensore *m*	ash-en-sor-ay
light	la luce	loo-chay
colour	chiaro	kee-ar-oh
weight	leggero	le-je-ro
lighter fuel	la benzina per accendisigaro	ben-zee-na pair ach-en-dee-see-ga-ro
lighthouse	il faro	fa-ro
like (to) *it pleases me*	mi piace	mee pee-a-chay
wish	volere	vo-lair-ay
line	la linea	lee-ne-a
linen	la tela	te-la
lingerie	la biancheria per signore	byan-ke-ree-a per seen-yo-ra
lipstick	il rossetto	ros-set-oh
liquid *adj.*	liquido	lee-kwee-doh
noun	il liquido	lee-kwee-doh
listen (to) *e*	ascoltare	as-kol-tar-ay
little *amount*	poco	poh-ko
size	piccolo	peek-koh-lo
live (to)	vivere	vee-vair-ay
local	locale	loh-ka-lay
lock	la serratura	ser-ra-too-ra

lock (to)	chiudere a chiave	**kyoo-de-ray a kee-a-vay**
long	lungo	**loon-go**
look (to) *at*	guardare	**gwar-dar-ay**
for	cercare	**chair-kar-ay**
like	sembrare	**sem-brar-ay**
lorry	il camion	**kam-ee-on**
lose (to)	perdere	**pair-dair-ay**
lost property office	gli oggetti smarriti	**oj-et-tee smar-ree-tee**
loud	forte	**for-tay**
love (to)	amare	**a-ma-ray**
lovely	bello	**bel-lo**
low	basso	**bas-so**
luggage	i bagagli	**bag-al-yee**
lunch	la colazione/ il pranzo	**ko-la-tsyo-nay/ prant-so**

M

magazine	la rivista	ree-vees-ta
maid	la cameriera	ka-mair-yair-a
mail	la posta	pos-ta

main street	la strada principale	stra-da preen-chee-pa-lay
make (to)	fare	far-ray
make love (to)	fare l'amore	fa-ray la-mo-ray
make-up	il trucco	trook-ko
male *adj.*	maschile	ma-shee-lay
man	l'uomo *m*	wom-oh
manage (to)	dirigere	dee-ree-je-ray
manager	il direttore	dee-ret-or-ay
manicure	la manicure	man-ee-koo-ray
many	molti	mol-tee
map *country*	la carta geografica	kar-ta je-o-gra-fee-ka
town, *small area*	la mappa	map-pa
market	il mercato	mair-ka-toh
market place	la piazza del mercato	pee-at-sa del mair-ka-toh
married	sposato	spo-za-toh
Mass	la messa	mes-sa
massage	il massaggio	mas-saj-jo
match *light*	il fiammifero	fee-am-mee-fair-oh
sport	la partita	par-tee-ta
material *fabric*	la stoffa	stof-fa
mattress	il materasso	mat-air-as-so
me	mi, me	mee, may

meal	il pasto	pas-toh
measurements	le misure	mee-zoo-ray
meet (to)	incontrare	een-kon-tra-ray
mend (to)	riparare	ree-par-ar-ay
mess	la confusione	kon-foo-syo-nay
message	il messaggio	mes-saj-jo
metal	il metallo	me-tal-oh
middle	centro, mezzo	chen-troh, med-zo
middle-aged	di mezza età	dee med-za e-ta
middle class *adj.*	borghese	bor-gay-say
noun	il ceto medio	che-toh med-yo
mild	mite	mee-tay
mine *pron.*	il mio/la mia; i miei/le mie	mee-oh/mee-a; mye-ee/mee-ay
minute	il minuto	mee-noo-toh
mirror	lo specchio	spek-yoh
Miss	signorina *f*	seen-yor-ee-na
miss (to) *train, etc.*	perdere	pair-dair-ay
mistake	lo sbaglio	zbal-yoh
mix (to)	mescolare	mes-ko-la-ray
mixed	mescolato/misto	mes-ko-la-toh/mees-toh
modern	moderno	mod-air-no
moment	il momento	mo-men-toh

money	il denaro	den-ar-oh
month	il mese	may-say
monument	il monumento	mo-noo-men-toh
moon	la luna	loo-na
more	(di) più	dee pyoo
morning	la mattina	mat-te-na
mosquito	la zanzara	zan-za-ra
most	il più/la più	pyoo
mother	la madre	ma-dray
motor boat	la motobarca	mo-toh-bar-ka
motor cycle	la motocicletta	mo-toh-chee-klet-ta
motor racing	la corsa automobilistica	kor-sa ow-toh-mo-bee-lees-tee-ka
motorway	l'autostrada	ow-toh-stra-da
mountain	la montagna	mon-tan-ya
mouth	la bocca	bok-ka
mouthwash	il colluttorio	kol-lot-tor-yo
move (to)	muovere	mwo-ve-ray
Mr	signor *m*	seen-yor
Mrs	signora *f*	seen-yora
much	molto	mol-toh
museum	il museo	moo-zay-oh
music	la musica	moo-zee-ka
must (*to have to*)	dovere	do-ve-ray

| my | mio | mee-oh |
| myself | io stesso | ee-yo stes-so |

N

nail *carpentry*	il chiodo	kyo-doh
finger	l'unghia *f*	oong-ya
nailbrush	lo spazzolino da unghie	spat-zo-lee-no
nailfile	la limetta da unghie	lee-met-ta
nail polish	lo smalto per unghie	smal-toh
name	il nome	no-may
napkin	il tovagliolo	toh-val-yoh-lo
nappy	il pannolino	pan-no-lee-no
narrow	stretto	stret-toh
near	vicino	vee-chee-no
nearly	quasi	kwa-see
necessary	necessario	nech-es-ar-yo
necklace	la collana	kol-la-na
need (to)	aver bisogno di	a-vairr bee-zon-yo dee
needle	l'ago *m*	a-go
never	mai	my
new	nuovo	nwo-vo
news	le notizie *f*	not-eets-yay

newspaper	il giornale	jor-nal-ay
next	prossimo	pross-ee-mo
nice	carino	kar-ee-no
nightclub	il locale notturno	lo-ka-lay not-toor-no
nightdress	la camicia da notte	ka-mee-cha da not-tay
nobody	nessuno	nais-soo-noh
noisy	rumoroso	roo-mor-oh-zo
none	nessuno	nais-soo-noh
north	nord *m*	norrd
not	non	non
note	il biglietto	beel-yet-toh
notebook	il taccuino	tak-wee-no
nothing	niente	nee-en-tay
notice	l'avviso *m*	av-vee-zoh
notice (to)	osservare	os-sair-var-ay
novel	il romanzo	ro-man-zoh
now	ora/adesso	o-ra/a-des-so
number	il numero	noo-mair-oh
nylon	il nailon	ny-lon

O

occasion	l'occasione *f*	ok-ka-syo-nay
occupation	l'occupazione *f*	ok-koo-pat-syo-nay
occupied	occupato	ok-koo-pa-toh
ocean	l'oceano *m*	oh-che-a-noh
odd *not even*	dispari	**dees**-pa-ree
strange	strano	stra-noh
of	di	dee
offer	l'offerta *f*	of-fair-ta
office	l'ufficio *m*	oof-fee-cho
official *adj.*	ufficiale	oof-fee-cha-lay
noun	l'ufficiale *m*	oof-fee-cha-lay
often	spesso	spes-so
ointment	l'unguento *m*	oon-gwen-toh
old	vecchio	vek-yo
on	su, sopra	soo, sop-ra
once	una volta	oo-na vol-ta
only	soltanto	sol-tan-toh
open (to)	aprire	ap-reer-ay
open *pp*	aperto	a-pair-toh
opening	l'apertura *f*	a-pair-too-ra
opera	l'opera *f*	op-air-a
opportunity	l'occasione *f*	ok-ka-syo-nay

opposite	opposto	op-pos-toh
or	o	oh
orchestra	l'orchestra *f*	or-kes-tra
order (to)	ordinare	or-dee-nar-ay
ordinary	solito	**sol**-ee-toh
other	altro	al-tro
ought	dovere	do-ve-ray
our, ours	nostro	nos-tro
out(side)	fuori	fwor-ee
out of order	guasto	gwas-toh
over	sopra	sop-ra
over there	là	la
overcoat	il soprabito	sop-ra-bee-toh
overnight	per la notte	per la not-tay
owe (to)	dovere	dov-air-ay
owner	il proprietario	prop-ree-et-ar-yo

P

pack (to)	impaccare	eem-pak-kar-ay
packet	il pacchetto	pak-ket-toh
page	la pagina	**pa**-jee-na
paid	pagato	pa-ga-toh

pain	il dolore	do-lor-ay
paint (to)	dipingere	dee-peen-jair-ay
painting	la pittura/	peet-too-ra/
	il quadro	kwad-ro
pair	il paio	pa-yoh
palace	il palazzo	pal-at-zo
pale	pallido	pal-lee-doh
paper	la carta	kar-ta
parcel	il pacco	pak-oh
park	il parco	par-ko
park (to)	parcheggiare	par-kej-jar-ay
part	la parte	par-tay
party *fête*	la festa	fes-ta
political	il partito	par-tee-toh
pass (to)	passare	pass-ar-ay
passenger	il passeggero	pas-saj-je-ro
passport	il passaporto	pas-sa-por-toh
past *adj.*	passato	pas-sa-toh
noun	il passato	pas-sa-toh
path	il sentiero	sent-yair-oh
patient	il paziente	pats-yen-tay
pavement	il marciapiede	mar-cha-pye-day
pay (to)	pagare	pa-ga-ray
peak	la cima	chee-ma

pearl	la perla	pair-la
pebble	il ciottolo	chot-to-lo
pedal	il pedale	pe-da-lay
pedestrian	il pedone	pe-doh-nay
(fountain) pen	la penna (stilografica)	pen-na (stee-lo-gra-fee-ka)
pencil	la matita	ma-tee-ta
penknife	il temperino	tem-pair-ee-no
people	la gente	jen-tay
perfect	esatto/perfetto	e-sat-toh/per-fet-toh
performance	lo spettacolo	spet-tak-oh-lo
perfume	il profumo	pro-foo-mo
perhaps	forse	for-say
perishable	deperibile	day-pair-ee-bee-lay
perm	la permanente	pair-man-en-tay
permit	il permesso	pair-mes-so
permit (to)	permettere	pair-met-tair-ay
person	la persona	pair-so-na
(per) person	a persona	a per-so-na
personal	personale	pair-so-nal-ay
petticoat	la sottana	sot-ta-na
photograph	la fotografia	foh-toh-graf-ee-a
photographer	il fotografo	foh-tog-ra-fo
piano	il pianoforte	pee-a-no-for-tay

pick (to) *choose*	scegliere	shel-ye-ray
gather, *pick up*	cogliere	kol-ye-ray
picnic	il picnic	peek-neek
piece	il pezzo	pet-zoh
pier	il molo	mo-lo
pillow	il guanciale	gwan-cha-lay
(safety) pin	lo spillo (di sicurezza)	speel-lo (de see-koo-ret-za)
pipe	la pipa	pee-pa
place	il posto	pos-toh
plain	semplice	sem-plee-chay
plan	il piano	pee-a-no
plant	la pianta	pyan-ta
plastic	plastica	plas-tee-ka
plate	il piatto	pee-at-toh
play *theatre*	la commedia	kom-may-dee-a
play (to)	giocare	jok-ar-ay
player	il giocatore	jo-ka-to-ray
please	per favore	pair fa-vor-ay
plenty of	molto, molti	mol-toh, mol-tee
pliers	le pinze	peent-say
plug *bath*	il tappo	tap-po
electric	la spina elettrica	spee-na el-et-tree-ka

pocket	la tasca	tas-ka
point	il punto	poon-toh
poisonous	velenoso	vay-lay-no-zo
police station	il commissariato di polizia	kom-mees-sa-ree-a-toh dee pol-eet-zee-a
policeman	il poliziotto	pol-eets-yot-oh
poor	povero	**poh**-vair-oh
pope	il papa	pa-pa
popular	popolare	pop-oh-lar-ay
port	il porto	por-toh
possible	possibile	pos-**see**-bee-lay
post (to)	imbucare	eem-boo-kar-ay
post box	la buca delle lettere	boo-ka del-lay let-tair-ay
post office	l'ufficio postale *m*	oo-fee-choh pos-ta-lay
postcard	la cartolina postale	kar-toh-lee-na pos-ta-lay
postman	il postino	pos-tee-no
postpone	rimandare	ree-man-da-ray
pound	la sterlina	stir-lee-na
(face) powder	la cipria	**chee**-pree-a
prefer (to)	preferire	pre-fair-eer-ay
prepare (to)	preparare	prep-ar-ar-ay
present *gift*	il regalo	ray-ga-lo

press (to)	premere	**pre**-mair-ay
pretty	carino	ka-ree-no
price	il prezzo	pret-zo
priest	il prete	pre-tay
print	la stampa	stam-pa
print (to)	stampare	stam-pa-ray
private	privato	pree-va-toh
problem	il problema	prob-lay-ma
profession	la professione	pro-fes-yoh-nay
programme	il programma	pro-gram-ma
promise	la promessa	pro-mes-sa
promise (to)	promettere	pro-met-te-ray
provide (to)	fornire	for-nee-ray
public	pubblico	**poob**-lee-ko
pull (to)	tirare	teer-ar-ay
pure	puro	poo-roh
purse	il borsellino	bor-sel-ee-no
push (to)	spingere	**speen**-jair-ay
put (to)	mettere	**met**-air-ay
pyjamas	il pigiama	pee-ja-ma

Q

quality	la qualità	kwa-lee-ta
quantity	la quantità	kwan-tee-ta
quarter	il quarto	kwar-toh
queen	la regina	re-jee-na
question	la domanda	doh-man-da
quick	presto	pres-toh
quiet	tranquillo	tran-kwee-lo

R

race	la corsa	kor-sa
racecourse	l'ippodromo *m*	eep-poh-droh-mo
radiator	il radiatore	rad-ya-tor-ay
radio	la radio	rad-yoh
railway	la ferrovia	fer-roh-vee-a
rain	la pioggia	pee-od-ja
raincoat	l'impermeabile *m*	eem-pair-may-a-bee-lay
(it is) raining	piove	pee-oh-vay
rare	raro	ra-roh
rather	piuttosto	pyoot-tos-toh
raw	crudo	kroo-doh

razor	il rasoio	raz-oy-oh
razor blade	la lametta per barba	lam-et-a pair bar-ba
reach (to)	raggiungere	raj-joon-je-ray
read (to)	leggere	led-jair-ay
ready	pronto	pron-toh
real	vero	vair-oh
really	veramente	vair-a-men-tay
reason	la ragione	ra-jo-nay
receipt	la ricevuta	ree-che-voo-ta
receive (to)	ricevere	ree-chay-vair-ay
recent	recente	re-chen-tay
recipe	la ricetta	ree-chet-ta
recognize (to)	riconoscere	ree-ko-no-she-ray
recommend	raccomandare	ra-ko-man-dar-ay
record *music*	il disco	dees-ko
refrigerator	il frigorifero	free-go-ree-fe-ro
registered letter	lettera raccomandata	lait-ter-a rak-ko-man-da-ta
relatives	i parenti	pa-ren-tee
religion	la religione	re-lee-jo-nay
remember (to)	ricordare	ree-kor-dar-ay
rent (to)	affittare	af-feet-ta-ray
repair (to)	riparare	ree-par-ar-ay
repeat (to)	ripetere	ree-pet-air-ay

reply (to)	rispondere	ree-spon-dair-ay
reservation	la prenotazione	pray-not-at-zee-oh-nay
reserve (to)	prenotare/ riservare	pray-not-ar-ay/ ree-zair-var-ay
reserved	prenotato	pray-not-a-toh
restaurant	il ristorante	rees-tor-an-tay
restaurant car	il vagone ristorante	va-go-nay rees-tor-an-tay
return (to)	ritornare	ree-tor-nar-ay
reward	la ricompensa	ree-kom-pen-sa
ribbon	il nastro	nas-tro
rich	ricco	reek-ko
right *opp. left*	destro	des-troh
opp. wrong	corretto	kor-ret-toh
right (to be)	aver ragione	a-vair ra-jo-nay
ring *finger*	l'anello *m*	an-el-oh
ripe	maturo	ma-too-ro
rise (to)	sorgere	sor-je-ray
river	il fiume	few-may
road	la strada	stra-da
roasted	arrosto	ar-oss-toh
rock	lo scoglio	skol-yo
roll *bread*	il panino	pan-ee-no

roll (to)	rotolare	ro-to-la-ray
rollers *hair*	i bigodini	bee-go-dee-nee
roof	il tetto	tet-toh
room	la stanza	stant-sa
rope	la fune	foo-nay
round	rotondo	ro-ton-doh
rowing boat	la barca a remi	bar-ka a ray-mee
rubber	la gomma	gom-ma
rubbish	le immondizie	ee-mon-deet-zee-ay
rucksack	il sacco da montagna	sak-ko da mon-tan-ya
run (to)	correre	kor-rair-ay
rush hour	l'ora di punta *f*	o-ra dee poon-ta

S

sad	triste	trees-tay
safe	sicuro	see-koo-ro
sailor	il marinaio	ma-ree-na-yo
sale *clearance*	la svendita	sven-dee-ta
(for) sale	in vendita	een ven-dee-ta
salesgirl	la commessa (di negozio)	kom-mess-a
salesman	il commesso (di negozio)	kom-mess-oh

salt	il sale	sa-lay
salt water	l'acqua salata *f*	ak-wa sa-la-ta
same	stesso	stess-oh
sand	la sabbia	sab-bya
sandals	i sandali	san-da-lee
sanitary towel	l'assorbente igienico *m*	ass-or-ben-tay eej-yen-ee-ko
satisfactory	soddisfacente	sod-dees-fa-chen-tay
saucer	il piattino	pee-at-tee-no
save (to) *money*	risparmiare	rees-par-mya-ray
rescue	salvare	sal-va-ray
say (to)	dire	dee-ray
scald (to)	scottare	skot-ar-ay
scarf	la sciarpa	shar-pa
scenery	il paesaggio	pa-ye-zaj-jo
scent	il profumo	pro-foo-mo
school	la scuola	skwo-la
scissors	le forbici	for-bee-chee
Scotland	Scozia *f*	skots-ya
Scottish	scozzese	skots-ay-zay
scratch (to)	graffiare	graf-fya-ray
screw	la vite	vee-tay
sculpture	la scultura	skool-too-ra
sea	il mare	ma-ray

sea food	i frutti di mare	froot-tee dee ma-ray
seasickness	il mal di mare	mal dee ma-ray
season	la stagione	sta-jo-nay
seat	il posto	pos-toh
second	secondo	se-kon-doh
see (to)	vedere	ved-air-ay
seem (to)	parere	par-air-ay
sell (to)	vendere	ven-dair-ay
send (to)	mandare	man-dar-ay
separate *adj*	a parte	a par-tay
serious	serio	sair-yoh
serve (to)	servire	sair-vee-ray
service	il servizio	sair-veetz-yo
service *church*	il servizio religioso	sair-veetz-yo rel-ee-jo-so
service charge	il servizio	sair-veetz-yo
several	parecchi	par-rek-ee
sew (to)	cucire	koo-cheer-ay
shade *colour*	la tinta	teen-ta
shade/shadow	l'ombra *f*	om-bra
shallow	basso	bass-oh
shampoo	lo shampoo	sham-po
shape	la forma	for-ma
share (to)	dividere	dee-vee-dair-ay

sharp	tagliente	tal-yen-tay
shave (to)	farsi la barba	far-see la bar-ba
shaving brush	il pennello	pen-ell-oh
shaving cream	la crema da barba	kray-ma da bar-ba
she	essa, lei	es-sa, lay
sheet	il lenzuolo	lentz-woh-lo
shell	la conchiglia	kon-cheel-ya
shelter	il riparo	ree-pa-ro
shine (to)	splendere	splen-dair-ay
shingle	i ciottoli	chot-oh-lee
ship	la nave	na-vay
shipping line	la compagnia di navigazione	kom-pan-yee-a dee na-vee-gatz-yo-nay
shirt	la camicia	kam-ee-cha
shock	il colpo	kol-po
shoe	la scarpa	skar-pa
shoelace	le stringhe da scarpe	streen-gay da skar-pay
shoe polish	la tinta da scarpe	teen-ta da skar-pay
shop	la bottega	bot-ay-ga
shopping centre	il centro dei negozi	chen-tro de-ee ne-got-see
shore	la spiaggia	spyaj-ja
short	corto	kor-toh
shorts	i calzoncini	kalt-zon-chee-nee

shoulder	la spalla	spal-la
show	lo spettacolo	spet-tak-oh-lo
show (to)	mostrare	mos-trar-ay
shower	la doccia	dot-cha
shut (to)	chiudere	kew-dair-ay
shut *pp*	chiuso	kew-zo
side	il lato	la-toh
sights	le vedute	ve-doo-tay
sightseeing	il giro turistico	jee-ro toor-ees-tee-ko
sign	il segno	sen-yo
sign (to)	firmare	feer-ma-ray
silk	la seta	say-ta
silver	l'argento *m*	ar-jen-toh
simple	semplice	sem-plee-chay
since	da	da
sing (to)	cantare	kan-ta-ray
single *just one*	singolo	seen-go-lo
unmarried	scapolo *of man*	ska-po-lo
	nubile *of woman*	noo-bee-lay
single room	la camera a un letto	ka-mair-a a oon let-toh
sister	la sorella	sor-rel-a
sit (to)	sedere	sed-air-ay
sit down (to)	accomodarsi	ak-om-oh-dar-see
size	la misura	mee-zoo-ra

skate (to)	pattinare	pat-tee-na-ray
ski (to)	sciare	shee-ar-ay
skid (to)	slittare	sleet-ar-ay
skirt	la gonna	gon-na
sky	il cielo	chee-ay-loh
sleep (to)	dormire	dor-meer-ay
sleeper	il vagone letto	va-go-nay let-oh
sleeping bag	il sacco a pelo	sa-koh a pe-lo
sleeve	la manica	ma-nee-ka
slice	la fetta	fet-ta
slip *garment*	la sottoveste	sot-toh-ves-tay
slippers	le pantofole/ le ciabotte	pan-tof-oh-lay/ chee-ab-at-tay
slowly	lentamente	len-ta-men-tay
small	piccolo	pee-koh-lo
smart	elegante	ele-gan-tay
smell	l'odore *m*	o-do-ray
smile	sorridere	sor-ree-de-ray
smoke (to)	fumare	foo-mar-ay
smoking (compartment)	(scompartimento) fumatori	(skom-par-tee-men-toh) foo-ma-tor-ee
no smoking	vietato fumare	vee-et-a-toh foo-mor-ay
snow	la neve	nay-vay

(it is) snowing	nevica	nay-vee-ka
so	così	ko-zee
soap	il sapone	sap-oh-nay
soap powder	il sapone in polvere	sap-oh-nay een pol-vair-ay
sober	sobrio	sob-ryo
socks	i calzini	kalt-zee-nee
soft	molle	mol-lay
sold	venduto	ven-doo-toh
sole *shoe*	la suola	swoh-la
solid	solido	so-lee-doh
some	qualche	kwal-kay
somebody	qualcuno	kwal-koo-no
something	qualcosa	kwal-ko-za
sometimes	qualche volta	kwal-kay vol-ta
somewhere	in qualche parte	een kwal-kay par-tay
son	il figlio	feel-yo
song	la canzone	kant-so-nay
soon	presto	pres-toh
sour	acido	a-chee-doh
south	sud *m*	sood
souvenir	il ricordo	ree-kor-doh
space	lo spazio	spat-zyo
spanner	la chiave	kya-vay

speak (to)	parlare	par-lar-ay
speciality	la specialità	spe-cha-lee-**ta**
spectacles	gli occhiali	ok-ya-lee
speed	la velocità	vel-oh-chee-**ta**
speed limit	il limite di velocità	lee-mee-tay dee vel-oh-chee-**ta**
spend (to)	spendere	spen-dair-ay
spoon	il cucchiaio	koo-ky-eye-oh
sport	lo sport	sporrt
sprain (to)	slogare	slo-ga-ray
spring *water*	la sorgente	sor-jen-tay
square *adj.*	quadrato	kwad-ra-toh
noun	la piazza	pee-at-za
stage	il palcoscenico	pal-ko-shen-ee-ko
stain	la macchia	mak-ya
stained	macchiato	mak-ya-toh
stairs	le scale	ska-lay
stalls	le poltrone	pol-tro-nay
stamp	il francobollo	fran-ko-bol-lo
stand (to)	stare in piedi	star-ay een pee-ay-dee
start (to)	cominciare	kom-een-char-ay
statue	la statua	stat-oo-a
stay (to)	stare	star-ay
step *foot*	il passo	pass-oh

stick	il bastone	bas-to-nay
stiff	rigido	ree-jee-doh
still	ancora	an-kor-a
not moving	immobile	eem-mo-bee-lay
sting	la puntura	poon-toor-a
stockings	le calze	kalt-zay
stolen	rubato	roo-ba-toh
stone	la pietra	pee-ay-tra
stool	lo sgabello	sga-bel-lo
stop (to)	fermare	fair-ma-ray
store	il magazzino	ma-ga-dzee-no
straight	diritto	dee-ree-toh
straight on	a diritto	a dee-ree-toh
strap	la cinghia	cheeng-ya
stream	il ruscello	roo-shell-oh
street	la strada	stra-da
string	lo spago	spa-go
strong	forte	for-tay
student	lo studente	stoo-den-tay
style	lo stile	stee-lay
suburb	la periferia	pair-ee-fair-ee-a
subway	il sottopassaggio	sot-toh-pass-adj-yo
suede	il camoscio	kam-ch-sho

suit	l'abito *m*	a-bee-toh
suitcase	la valigia	va-lee-ja
sun	il sole	so-lay
sunbathing	il bagno di sole	ban-yoh dee so-lay
sunburn	la scottatura di sole	skot-at-oo-ra dee so-lay
sunglasses	gli occhiali da sole	ok-ya-lee da so-lay
sunhat	il cappello da sole	ka-pell-oh da so-lay
sunny	soleggiato	so-lej-ja-toh
sunshade	il parasole	pa-ra-so-lay
suntan cream	la pomata solare	po-ma-ta so-la-ray
supper	la cena	chay-na
sure	sicuro	see-koo-ro
surgery	l'ambulatorio *m*	am-boo-la-tor-ee-oh
surprise	la sorpresa	sor-pre-sa
surprise (to)	sorprendere	sor-pren-de-ray
suspender belt	le giarrettiere	jar-ret-yair-ay
sweater	il maglione	mal-yo-nay
sweet	dolce	dol-chay
sweets	le caramelle	ka-ra-mel-lay
swell (to)	gonfiare	gon-fee-ar-ay
swim (to)	nuotare	nwo-tar-ay
swimming pool (open)	la piscina (all' aperto)	pee-shee-na (al-la-per-toh)

| swings | l'altalena *f* | al-ta-le-na |
| switch *light* | l'interruttore *m* | een-tair-roo-tor-ay |

T

table	la tavola	ta-voh-la
tablecloth	la tovaglia	toh-val-ya
tablet	la pastiglia	pas-teel-ya
tailor	il sarto	sar-toh
take (to)	prendere	pren-dair-ay
talk (to)	parlare	par-lar-ay
tall	alto	al-toh
tank	il serbatoio	ser-ba-toy-oh
tap	il rubinetto	roo-bee-net-oh
taste	il gusto	goos-toh
taste (to)	gustare	goos-ta-ray
tax	la tassa	tass-a
taxi	il tassì	tas-see
teach (to)	insegnare	een-sen-yar-ay
tear *eye*	la lacrima	la-kree-ma
tear (to)	strappare	strap-pa-ray
telegram	il telegramma	te-le-gram-a
telephone	il telefono	te-le-foh-no
telephone (to)	telefonare	te-le-fon-ar-ay

telephone box	la cabina telefonica	ka-bee-na te-le-fon-ee-ka
telephone call	la telefonata	te-le-fon-a-ta
telephone directory	l'elenco telefonico *m*	el-en-koh te-le-fon-ee-ko
telephone number	il numero di telefono	noo-mair-oh dee te-le-fon-oh
telephone operator	il centralino	chen-tra-lee-noh
television	il televisore	te-le-vee-zor-ay
tell (to)	raccontare	rak-on-tar-ay
temperature	la temperatura	tem-pair-at-oo-ra
temporary	provvisorio	prov-vee-sor-yo
tennis	il tennis	ten-nees
tent	la tenda	ten-da
tent peg	il cavicchio per tenda	ka-veek-yo pair ten-da
tent pole	il palo per tenda	pa-lo pair ten-da
terrace	la terrazza	ter-rat-za
than	che, di	kay, dee
that	quello	kwell-oh
the	il, lo, la; i, gli, le	eel, oh, la; ee, lly-ee, lay
theatre	il teatro	tay-at-ro
their, theirs	loro	lor-oh
them	li, loro	lee, lor-oh
then	poi, allora	poy, al-or-a

there	lì, là	lee, la
there is	c'è	che
there are	ci sono	chee so-no
thermometer	il termometro	tair-mom-et-ro
these	questi	kwes-tee
they	essi	es-see
thick	grosso	gross-oh
thin	sottile	sot-ee-lay
thing	la cosa	ko-sa
think (to)	pensare	pen-sar-ay
thirsty (to be)	aver sete	a-vair say-tay
this	questo	kwes-toh
those	quelli	kwel-ee
thread	il filo	fee-lo
throat	la gola	go-la
through	attraverso	at-tra-vair-so
throw (to)	gettare	jet-tar-ay
thunderstorm	la tempesta	tem-pes-ta
ticket	il biglietto	beel-yet-oh
tide	la marea	ma-ray-a
tie	la cravatta	kra-vat-ta
tight	attillato	at-teel-a-toh
time	il tempo	tem-po
timetable	l'orario m	or-ar-yo

tin	il barattolo	ba-ra-toh-lo
tin opener	l'apriscatole *m*	a-pree-**skat**-oh-lay
tip *money*	la mancia	man-cha
(to) *money*	dare una mancia	da-ray oo-na man-cha
tired	stanco	stan-ko
to	a, in	a, een
tobacco (brown)	il tabacco (scuro)	ta-ba-koh (skoo-roh)
tobacco pouch	la borsa da tabacco	bor-sa da ta-ba-ko
together	insieme	een-see-ay-may
toilet	il gabinetto	ga-bee-net-oh
toilet paper	la carta igienica	kar-ta eej-**yen**-ee-ka
tongue	la lingua	leen-gwa
too *also*	anche	an-kay
excessive	troppo	trop-po
too much/many	troppo/troppi	trop-po/trop-pee
toothbrush	lo spazzolino da denti	spat-so-lee-no da den-tee
toothpaste	il dentifricio	den-tee-free-cho
toothpick	lo stuzzicadenti	stoots-ee-ka-den-tee
top	la cima	chee-ma
torch *electric*	la lampadina tascabile	lam-pa-dee-na tas-ka-bee-lay
torn	strappato	strap-pa-toh
touch (to)	toccare	tok-ar-ay

tough	duro	doo-ro
tourist	il turista	toor-ees-ta
towards	verso	vair-so
towel	l'asciugamano *m*	ash-yoo-ga-ma-no
tower	la torre	tor-ray
town	la città	cheet-ta
town hall	il municipio	moo-nee-chee-pyo
toy	il giocattolo	jok-at-oh-lo
traffic	il traffico	traf-ee-ko
traffic jam	l'ingorgo di traffico *m*	een-gor-go dee traf-fee-ko
traffic lights	il semaforo	sem-af-or-oh
train	il treno	tray-no
transfer	trasferire	tras-fe-ree-ray
translate (to)	tradurre	trad-oor-ray
travel (to)	viaggiare	vee-ad-jar-ay
travel agent	l'agenzia di viaggi *f*	agent-see-a dee vee-ad-jee
traveller	il viaggiatore	vee-ad-ja-tor-ay
travellers' cheque	l'assegno turistico *m*	ass-en-yoh toor-ees-tee-ko
treat (to)	trattare	trat-ta-ray
medical	curare	ko-ra-ray
treatment	la cura	koo-ra
tree	l'albero *m*	al-bair-oh

trip	il viaggio	vee-ad-jo
trouble	il guaio	goo-eye-oh
trousers	i pantaloni	pan-ta-lo-nee
true	vero	vair-oh
trunk *luggage*	il baule	bow-lay
trunks	i calzoncini	kalt-zon-chee-nee
truth	la verità	ve-ree-ta
try, try on (to)	provare	pro-var-ay
tunnel	la galleria	gal-air-ee-a
turn (to)	voltare	vol-tar-ay
turning	la svolta	svol-ta
tweezers	le pinzette	peent-set-tay
twisted	slogato	slo-ga-toh

U

ugly	brutto	broo-toh
umbrella	l'ombrello *m*	om-brell-oh
uncle	lo zio	tsee-oh
uncomfortable	scomodo	**scom**-oh-doh
under	sotto	sot-toh
underground	la metropolitana	met-roh-pol-lee-ta-na
underneath	sotto	sot-toh
understand	capire	ka-peer-ay

underwear	la biancheria intima	bee-ank-air-ee-a een-tee-ma
university	l'università *f*	oo-nee-vair-see-ta
unpack (to)	disfare le valigie	dees-far-ay lay val-ee-gay
until	fino a	fee-no a
unusual	insolito	een-sol-ee-toh
up	sopra	sop-ra
upstairs	di sopra	dee sop-ra
urgent	urgente	oor-jen-tay
us	noi, ci	noy, chee
use (to)	usare	oo-zar-ay
useful	utile	oo-tee-lay
useless	inutile	een-oo-tee-lay
usual	solito	sol-ee-toh

V

vacant	libero	lee-bair-oh
vacation	la vacanze	va-kant-say
valid	valido	va-lee-doh
valley	la valle	val-lay
valuable	di valore	dee va-lor-ay
value	la valuta	va-loo-ta

vase	il vaso	va-zo
vegetables	la verdura	vair-door-a
vegetarian	vegetariano	ve-je-tar-ya-no
ventilation	la ventilazione	ven-tee-latz-yo-nay
very	molto	mol-toh
very little	pochissimo	po-kee-see-mo
very much	moltissimo	mol-tee-see-mo
vest	la maglietta	mal-yet-a
viaduct	il viadotto	vee-a-dot-toh
view	la vista	vees-ta
village	il villaggio	vee-lad-jo
violin	il violino	vee-oh-lee-no
visa	il visto	vees-toh
visit	la visita	vee-zee-ta
visit (to)	visitare	vee-zee-ta-ray
voice	la voce	voh-chay
voltage	il voltaggio	vol-tad-jo
voyage	il viaggio	vee-ad-jo

wait (to)	aspettare	as-pet-ar-ay
waiter	il cameriere	ka-mair-yair-ay
waiting room	la sala d'aspetto	sa-la das-pet-oh

waitress	la cameriera	ka-mair-yair-a
wake (to) *someone*	svegliare	zvel-yar-say
wake up (to)	svegliarsi	zvel-yar-see
Wales	Galles *m*	gal-es
walk (to)	passeggiare	pass-ed-jar-ay
wallet	il portafoglio	por-ta-fol-yo
want (to)	volere	vo-lair-ay
wardrobe	il guardaroba	gwar-da-roh-ba
warm	caldo	kal-doh
wash (to)	lavare	la-var-ay
washbasin	il lavandino	la-van-dee-no
waste	il rifiuto	ree-fyoo-toh
waste (to)	sprecare	spre-ka-ray
watch	l'orologio *m*	or-oh-lo-jo
water	l'acqua *f*	ak-wa
waterfall	la cascata	kas-ka-ta
waterproof	impermeabile	eem-pair-me-abee-lay
water ski-ing	lo sci nautico	shee now-tee-ko
wave	l'onda *f*	on-da
way	la via	vee-a
we	noi	noy
wear (to)	indossare	een-doss-ar-ay
weather	il tempo	tem-po
week	la settimana	set-ee-ma-na

weigh (to)	pesare	pe-zar-ay
weight	il peso	pe-so
well *adv.*	bene	bay-nay
Welsh	gallese	gal-ay-zay
west	ovest *m*	oh-vest
wet	bagnato	ban-ya-toh
what?	che cosa?	kay ko-sa
wheel	la ruota	rwo-ta
when?	quando?	kwan-doh
where?	dove?	doh-vay
which?	quale?	kwa-lay
while	mentre	men-tray
who?	chi?	kee
whole	intero	een-tair-oh
whose?	di chi?	dee kee
why?	perchè?	pair-**kay**
wide	largo	lar-go
widow	la vedova	vay-doh-va
widower	il vedovo	vay-doh-vo
wife	la moglie	mol-yay
wild	selvaggio	sel-vaj-jo
win (to)	vincere	veen-chair-ay
wind	il vento	ven-toh
window	la finestra	fee-nes-tra

wing	l'ala *f*	a-la
wish (to)	desiderare	de-zee-dair-ar-ay
with	con	kon
without	senza	sen-za
woman	la donna	don-na
wood *forest*	il bosco	bos-ko
timber	il legno	len-yo
wool	la lana	la-na
word	la parola	pa-ro-la
work	il lavoro	la-vo-ro
work (to)	lavorare	la-vo-ra-ray
worried	preoccupato	pre-ok-koo-pa-toh
worse	peggiore	ped-jor-ay
worth (to be)	valore	va-lor-ay
wrap	avvolgere	a-vol-jair-ay
write (to)	scrivere	scree-vair-ay
writing paper	la carta da scrivere	kar-ta da scree-vair-ay
wrong	sbagliato	sbal-ya-toh
wrong (to be)	aver torto	a-vair tor-toh

Y

yacht	lo yacht	yat
year	l'anno *m*	an-no
you	voi, Lei	voy, lay
young	giovane	jo-van-ay
your	vostro/Suo	vos-tro/soo-oh
youth hostel	l'ostello della gioventù *m*	os-tell-oh del-la joh-ven-**too**

Z

| zip | la chiusura lampo | kew-zoo-ra lam-po |
| zoo | il giardino zoologico | jar-dee-no zoh-oh-lo-jee-ko |

Index